Updating
CLASSIC AMERICA
BUNGALOWS

Updating
CLASSIC AMERICA
BUNGALOWS

Design Ideas for Renovating, Remodeling, and Building New

M. Caren Connolly
and Louis Wasserman

The Taunton Press

The Taunton Press
Inspiration for hands-on living®

The Taunton Press, Inc., 63 South Main Street, PO Box 5506, Newtown, CT 06470-5506
e-mail: tp@taunton.com

Distributed by Publishers Group West

EDITOR: Roger Yepsen
DESIGN AND LAYOUT: Lori Wendin
ILLUSTRATOR: Louis Wasserman
COVER PHOTOGRAPHER: Rob Karosis

LIBRARY OF CONGRESS CATALOGING-IN-PUBLICATION DATA:
Connolly, M. Caren.
    Bungalows : design ideas for renovating, remodeling, and
building new / M. Caren Connolly and Louis Wasserman.
        p. cm. -- (Updating classic America)
    Includes index.
    ISBN 1-56158-435-5
    1. Bungalows--United States--Designs and plans.
I. Wasserman, Louis. II. Title. III. Series.
NA7571.C73 2002
728'.373'022273--dc21

2002007108

The following brand names/manufacturers are trademarks: Heinz™, Jacuzzi®, Palm™ Pilot, Volvo™

Printed in the United States of America
10 9 8 7 6 5 4 3

For Elizabeth, Eugene, and Eero, our sources of energy, inspiration, and delight, and to the memory of our friend Karen Beatty, who graced our lives with her intellect and vivacity.

Acknowledgments

HALFWAY THROUGH WRITING THIS BOOK we joked with our editor that we felt as though we were going to graduate school again. The learning curve in writing each book is tremendous, and we enjoy the daily challenge of learning something new and meeting deadlines. We would like to thank all of our "professors" at The Taunton Press: Jim Childs, Peter Chapman, Paula Schlosser, Carol Kasper, Carol Singer, Suzanne Noel, Brandi Gabriele, and Robyn Aitken. Special thanks to Steve Culpepper, formerly of The Taunton Press, who was our first Taunton contact, and to our editor, Roger Yepsen.

Rob Karosis, the principal photographer, not only shared his talent to make the book come alive but generously shared his knowledge of photography with our oldest son. One of the brilliant fall days that Rob was in Milwaukee was September 11, 2001. As we shared dinner in our Bungalow that night, Rob's calm presence and underlying sense of light that comes through so clearly in his photographs helped our family through that dark time.

The homeowners, architects, and contractors who shared their stories (and their homes) with us should go to the head of the class. The people who inhabit, design, and construct these homes are the true hallmark of the Bungalow style.

CONTENTS

INTRODUCTION

When we first told friends, family, and other architects that we were writing a book about Bungalows, the typical response was formed by their geographic location. "Oh! Berkeley Bungalows!" Or, "I just love the Chicago Bungalow." Everyone seemed to think that the Bungalow was a housing style particular (and dear) to their own region. When we went on to explain that our book would profile Bungalows all over the country, including new Bungalows, they were surprised. Surprised and a little perplexed. "What exactly is a Bungalow?" was the next (and immediate) question.

A ubiquitous housing type, Bungalows are accepted more as a backdrop to the residential landscape than they are understood as an architectural style. We hope the examples in the following chapters will show that the beauty of the Bungalow style is that it is a universal housing type as well as a vernacular architecture, responsive to its site and context.

We moved to Milwaukee after many years of bouncing back and forth between the two coasts. Growing up, Louis lived in a beautifully detailed and compact modern house, designed by his architect father. From an early age he appreciated excellent craftsmanship, respect for materials, and deep community roots. Caren's experience as an "Army brat" was much different. Her housing experiences varied from living in converted barracks in Carlisle, Pennsylvania, and a cottage in Carmel, California, to a villa in Phnom Penh, Cambodia.

But we both knew what we wanted for our first home. We wanted a Bungalow.

Louis appreciated the attention to detail and the flexibility of the plan. As an architect, he knew that he could knock out a few walls and not lose the integrity of the Bungalow style. Caren appreciated the Bungalow neighborhoods, with their sense of place. The Realtor appreciated that she had two people who wanted to look at the 50 Bungalows listed with her agency. As is the case with many Bungalow families, we moved in, refinished the floors, remodeled the bathroom, added a bath, and contemplated moving. Somehow, like many Bungalow families, we have never gotten around to making that move.

Low to the ground and centered, Bungalows tend to weather fashion trends better than other housing types. Never known as status symbols, they are quiet, comfortable, delightful, and enduring. They grow on you and change with you. We really enjoyed telling the stories of the owners of the Bungalows in this book, and we look forward to inspiring people to explore all the opportunities Bungalows offer for creating a house that celebrates individual families while being a wonderful neighbor.

CHAPTER ONE

BUNGALOWS ARE BACK

ABOVE, **The Bungalow celebrates** the ways in which wood elements frame the house, often exposing the rafters, joists, and braces that other styles conceal. This detail from the fireplace of a new Bungalow is in that same spirit of honest joinery.

FACING PAGE, **The dormer windows** hint at the intimate rooms under the Bungalow roof.

I N AN AGE WHEN TEARDOWNS, scrape-offs, and wrap-arounds are radically altering the residential land-scape and "McMansions" are the prevailing crop of our farm fields, people are awakening to the value of traditional American neighborhoods. Many of us are returning to what can be called classic American hous-ing types—the Bungalow, the Colonial, the Cape, and the Ranch. We are drawn to their attention to materi-als, to details that would be prohibitively expensive today, and to attractive neighborhoods located close to downtown and mass-transit lines. These are communi-ties where kids can go to local schools and ride their bikes to the library or baseball diamond. Adults walk to the grocery store and post office and chat with neigh-bors along the way.

We're living in an era where most of us thrive on cutting-edge technology—Palm™ Pilots, e-mail, laptop computers, fax machines, car phones, split-screen televi-sions, microwaves, cell phones, and digital cameras. And yet we're clamoring to drive home each night to neigh-borhoods that are a step back in time. Americans never

Brick is the most common building material for Chicago's many Bungalows. The fronts of these houses often are high-quality face brick, while the rear is common brick.

really have embraced Modern architecture when it comes to homes. The last new style to sweep the country was the Ranch of the 1950s and '60s, and since then, houses have taken a decidedly revisionist turn.

And now the humble Bungalow has arrived—again. After having been overlooked for several decades, the Bungalow-style house is making a resurgence. Because of the style's relatively small size, prospective buyers used to drive right by these homes at Sunday open houses. It seemed everyone wanted a new four-bedroom, center-entrance home. Now, as with most things, the Bungalow has come full circle, and people again are looking for homes with character, detail, and a layout that makes sense. Classified ads take care to mention the

style by name, and rising prices testify to its renewed popularity. Here in Milwaukee, the assessment of our own Bungalow went up a remarkable 46 percent in just one year. The reason? According to a statement made by the town assessor, "The increase in valuation was the result of strong competition for the Bungalow-type home that has been a sort of phenomenon for the past few years." Bungalows remain a good value when you consider their flexibility, potential, and location.

An Ideal Home for America

The appeal of the Bungalow is the same now as it was 100 years ago. At a glance, you can appreciate the solidity, a sense of security, and a relationship with other houses along the street. Inside, the rooms are arranged in a way that reinforces family togetherness, with easy access to the yard to encourage outdoor living. On closer inspection, you can appreciate the warmth of the wood trim and a quality of finish that seems like something out the past.

Of course any older house is apt to need work. Perhaps because Bungalows tend to come with such well-crafted trim, many families enjoy taking part in the patient tasks of restoration, such as stripping paint and old varnish from woodwork and built-in cabinetry. This may be all a home needs to bring it back to life. Other Bungalows go through structural changes, as the floor plan is reconfigured or the walls and roof are pushed this way and that. The challenge here is to adapt the house sensitively so that its distinctive character isn't lost. And in a number of places around the country, new Bungalows are springing up for the first time in over half a century.

ABOVE, **The owners of this Washington State Bungalow** found French doors at an architectural salvage warehouse. The doors had to be stripped, sanded, varnished, and reglazed, but now they look as though they've always been there.

LEFT, **The typical modern suburban house,** with its broad lawn and metal front door, does little to welcome visitors. This Bungalow speaks of a friendlier time— one that many homeowners seek to keep alive today.

A Street of Bungalows

☆ **BUNGALOWS ARE COMPATIBLE** with one another because each is a variation on a theme rather than a radical, jarring departure. This is good to keep in mind when planning alterations to a Bungalow. Even subtle changes will be enough to distinguish your house, without running the risk of making it discordant.

Below is a rich neighborhood streetscape made up of just three versions of a basic Bungalow plan. The signature Bungalow elements are used in different ways to avoid the cookie-cutter look of many developments.

ATTRACTIONS OF THE BUNGALOW

Back when "Bungalow Mania," as it was called, introduced thousands to homeownership, the style was more than the fashion of the day. It incorporated a number of progressive ideals of the early 1900s—the straightforward use of materials, an informal way of living, and accessibility to the outdoors. The first Bungalow owners were interested in affordable homes that would both simplify their lives and allow them to enjoy the outdoors as part of their daily routines. Most were middle-class families who felt secure enough about their social standing that they didn't need to use shelter as an outward display of their worth.

Today, people are again attracted to homes of an appropriate size, built with honest materials. The Bungalow fits the bill, while offering such extras as oak floors, stained-glass windows, bay windows, coffered ceilings, wainscoting, brick and tile fireplaces, kitchen built-ins, and substantial frame-and-panel doors. Exterior details vary from one home to another, so that it is rare to find any two Bungalows that look exactly

ABOVE AND FACING PAGE, **In most Bungalows,** the porch is an integral part of the house so that indoor/outdoor living spaces are naturally woven together. A porch sends a friendly message to the neighborhood—like a welcome mat, only a lot more obvious.

Original Bungalow interiors were characterized by an entire catalog of distinctive materials, colors, shapes, and decorative themes. Oak was the favored wood, and dark stains predominated. The tapered angle of this mantel clock could also be seen on porch pillars and bookshelves. The vase, with its Art Nouveau landscape vignette, is an example of the handcrafted pottery that was prized in the period.

alike. Still, the houses along a street relate to each other in scale and materials, resulting in some of America's most charming neighborhoods.

Bungalow Hallmarks

While most Bungalows of the past had second-floor bedrooms, with dormers to bring in light and to increase headroom, the homes were meant to look like one-story structures with a strong visual connection to the site. The heavy roof overhang, supported by squat columns and braces, intentionally cast a strong shadow to emphasize this ground-hugging aspect. A great number of these homes had front porches that were integral to the architecture.

Exterior Hallmarks

AS WITH ANY STYLE, the Bungalow has a number of hallmarks by which it can be identified from the street. These typical features can be your guide when planning a restoration or renovation and will give the Bungalow flavor to your new home. Note that there is no need to slavishly include every element—you often see Bungalows that have omitted certain features while adding others. After all, the style came about in response to the need for affordable, healthful, and appealing housing. The Bungalow is more the product of a functional need than an abstract design philosophy and has always been freely adapted by owners, builders, and architects.

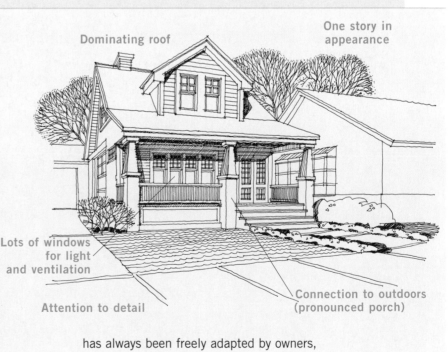

Dominating roof

One story in appearance

Lots of windows for light and ventilation

Attention to detail

Connection to outdoors (pronounced porch)

Even though Bungalow plans were often ordered from catalogs, reinforcing their shared characteristics, the style is highly adaptable. Builders of the original Bungalows favored regional materials for their lower cost and reduced maintenance. An unforeseen benefit of this restricted range of local options is that Bungalow neighborhoods have a coherent look about them.

If you live on the West Coast, you may notice the Mission influence of employing stucco as a primary building material. As you travel north, wood and brick become predominant. Chicago Bungalows tend to be yellow brick, while further north in Milwaukee the brick is generally a dark red hue. In the Northeast, shingles were often used to sheathe bays and gable ends. Of course, there are always exceptions to the rule. Here in our Milwaukee neighborhood, we enjoy the incongruent sight of two Mission Bungalows, one bright pink and one loud orange.

TRADITIONAL HOME, TRADITIONAL DESIGN

As every real estate agent will tell you, the three most compelling features of a home are location, location, and location, and Bungalows are often found in particularly attractive, established neighborhoods. The majority of them were built on the edge of downtown areas and in first-tier suburbs, in a day when social reformers were loudly describing urban ills. Of course, real estate developers were eager to accommodate the rush to flee apartment living.

A century later, Bungalow owners continue to appreciate this pedestrian-friendly environment, where the sidewalks are a great place to bump into people of all ages and catch up on neighborhood news. Getting to work or to stores is as easy as walking to the corner and catching the bus. For teenagers who are too young

While the principal reason to erect a dormer is to afford more headroom, Bungalow dormers were always trimmed out attractively, in keeping with the rest of the house. This one offers a panoramic view as well.

to drive, the independence of getting around on foot is especially appealing.

Bungalow neighborhoods tend to have a good mix of ages and family types, testifying to the style's wide appeal. Residents include many first-time homeowners moving from apartments. Bungalows are also logical choices for people downsizing from large homes in newer suburbs; these may be empty nesters looking for a condominium alternative, with small yards that allow spending time with friends and family instead of mowing the lawn.

Bungalows are suited to a variety of sites and climates, and their floor plans can accommodate anything from a historically faithful renovation to additions that literally go right through the roof. The style's adaptability can be explained in part by what it lacks: redundant walls and useless space. The open plan of the first floor

was a departure from the compartmentalized Victorian home, allowing rooms to have overlapping functions. And the Bungalow made excellent use of relatively few square feet. Many of today's home buyers are drawn by these assets, in a housing market dominated by huge houses with wasteful floor plans; they have found that a few thousand extra square feet does not necessarily mean having more useful room or enjoying greater comfort. The Bungalow owners we've worked with tell us they enjoy every square foot of their homes.

HUMILITY, THRIFT, AND EFFICIENCY

Bungalows are characterized by relatively little conspicuous ornamentation. Much as Ernest Hemingway's writing of the 1920s trimmed away the adjectives that Victorians had reveled in, the Bungalow pared down the embellishments of earlier architectural styles.

Bungalows, Squat and Not So Squat

WHAT EXACTLY IS A BUNGALOW? Even people who have lived in them for years may not be sure. Strictly speaking, a Bungalow is a one-story structure—or one that appears that way from the street—with a dominating roof that frames a welcoming porch. A Semi-Bungalow is a story-and-a-half in appearance but has a partial second story of space under those dormers in the roof. And the oddly named Bungaloid looks much like the others but is a full two stories high.

| Bungalow | Semi-Bungalow or Bungalow and a Half | Bungaloid (Two Stories) |

In a holdover from earlier styles, Bungalow woodwork often was stained dark. The effect calls attention to elaborate trim. Today's homeowners often prefer wood—oak, maple, or fir— to have a more natural finish, to be lighter and brighter.

Detailing is largely reserved for the entry, living room, and dining room, where visitors are received and the family gathers; these spaces are clearly meant to be the heart of daily life. Front doors and windows are rarely "off the shelf" stock items. The door might be massively crafted of oak with a graceful arch or a cherry construction flanked by sidelights. The one showy feature is apt to be windows of stained or beveled glass, often in intricately assembled designs.

Walk inside a Bungalow, and you'll note attention to craftsmanship in the crown moldings, baseboards, wainscoting, and wood floors. Whether the entry foyer is the size of a small room or little more than an elaborate threshold, it is treated as an essential space for greeting friends. Typically, living rooms include a decorative or working fireplace with glass-enclosed bookshelves; some homes have intimate built-in seating

Although original Bungalow owners thought of themselves as being very much up with the times, certain aspects of interior design wear well in almost any style. Wainscoting is a perennial favorite.

New construction fits right in with the existing house when care is taken to use traditional materials, such as the oak, tile, and brick in this fireplace.

arrangements known as **inglenooks.** We have found that these rooms invite reading, conversation, and board games, so that a family is less likely to rely on television and video games.

The centerpiece of the dining room is apt to be a built-in china cabinet and buffet. This fixture's very presence speaks of family gatherings and hospitality, and it epitomizes the marriage of efficiency and art. Drawers and cabinets provide convenient storage for china, silver, and linens. The mirror in the buffet makes the room appear larger and lighter, and beveled or stained glass in its doors adds ornamentation without compromising function.

inglenook — A recessed space for a fireplace, with built-in benches or wing chairs on either side of a fireplace.

☆ bungalow style

Interior Hallmarks

IT DOESN'T TAKE many interior design features to make a room fit comfortably within a Bungalow. And the trim doesn't have to be stained dark to make it qualify as true to the period; if you prefer a natural finish or to paint every last strip of wood, then you should feel free to do so. The original trim really wasn't so dark to begin with but has naturally darkened with age.

Generally, adding a lot of trim to a room will have the visual effect of unifying the walls and lowering the ceiling, making it seem more intimate—or cramped, if the trim is dark and the room is quite small.

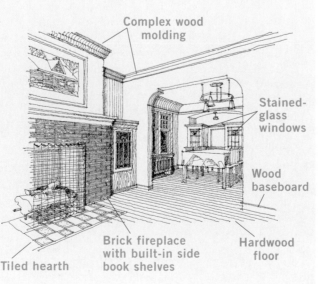

Complex wood molding

Stained-glass windows

Wood baseboard

Tiled hearth

Brick fireplace with built-in side book shelves

Hardwood floor

FACING PAGE, **To give some degree of separation** between living room and dining room, Bungalows often made use of partial walls with one or more pillars. In many homes, the low wall does double duty as cabinet space.

The Bungalow may be the coziest of any house style, with its small scale, inglenooks, generous use of wood, and window seats.

By placing importance on these family areas, the Bungalow helped to break down the rigid zoning that segregated Victorian households. In that earlier period, the husband had his private library, the wife was in charge of the children and the domestics, and the children were relegated to their own rooms. The Bungalow, on the other hand, has an informality that encourages togetherness and relaxed family roles.

Birth of the Bungalow

The Bungalow has informality in its bloodlines. The style's lineage is surprisingly exotic. The term itself is derived from the Hindi *bangala,* a one-story house with a low, extended roof that created a shady, well-ventilated veranda for outdoor living. When the British occupied India, they often summered in bangalas situated in cooler "hill station" towns where the high elevation provided relief from both the heat and the social stuffiness of the city. Over time, the style's basic form migrated to the United Kingdom. According to Anthony King, in *The Bungalow: The Production of a Global*

Bungalow Mysteries

AN EARLY NANCY DREW BOOK, *The Mystery in the Bungalow,* featured a Bungalow as the setting for Nancy's brilliant sleuthing. Agatha Christie wrote a mystery entitled *The Affair at the Bungalow.* Even though the Bungalow was not a major character in either story, the use of the term in the title suggests that Bungalows were an acknowledged style that would set a conventionally domestic scene for the reader.

☆ Period Lighting

BUNGALOWS MAY HAVE BEEN the first new houses to come electrified, and their original fixtures—both hard-wired and plug-in—were an important part of the style's appeal. In most cases, lamps were low power, casting a subtle glow that suggested lantern light. Shades of mica or amber glass tamed any glare from the incandescent bulbs. Stained-glass shades were splashier, but they didn't "shout" because their wattage was modest compared to today's light levels.

Many lamps appeared to be handcrafted brass, whether or not that was the case; on some, the rivets were for decoration only. In Craftsman Bungalows, hanging fixtures and wall sconces often were made to look like vintage lanterns, and yet electricity was held in such awe by early Bungalow owners that some rooms were lit by bare bulbs screwed into ceiling sockets. For more light, kitchens might have hanging Holophane lamps, with their bell-like shades of finely ribbed glass.

Perhaps because electric lighting was a novelty at the time, Bungalow fixtures were selected much like art objects, and care should be taken in choosing reproductions for your home.

Culture (1984), the first Western Bungalow was built in Kent in the late 1860s, no doubt as the home of a British colonial fresh from a tour of duty in India.

Like most popular housing styles in the United States, the Bungalow came to us via the United Kingdom. Architectural journals in the late 1800s make brief mention of Bungalows on Cape Cod, but it wasn't until early in the next century that the Bungalow caught on. Bungalow colonies became popular vacation destinations in mountain and seaside resorts, and Bungalows even appeared as settings in mystery stories, a favorite vacation reading genre.

Photographs from the period show that early American vacation Bungalows were often flimsily built. All of the rooms were on one floor, with sleeping

porches and tentlike overhanging roofs similar to those of the Indian bangala. The bangala's emphasis on outdoor living spaces was particularly suited to California's temperate climate, and the style first flourished in suburban Los Angeles. The area's trolley lines and a large influx of new residents also helped make the Bungalow an obvious choice for homeowners there. In Boise, Idaho, so many Bungalows were built in a short time that it was nicknamed Bungalow City. In the less forgiving climates of the Plains, the Midwest, and the Northeast, Bungalows were adapted by adding porches and sunrooms to capture the sunlight and offer a view. Bungalows were built in almost every state of the Union and across Canada, the vast concentration of them between 1900 and 1930.

ABOVE, **To ensure** that this sunroom fits in with the Bungalow style, the homeowners wisely chose to use closely spaced traditional double-hung windows rather than more contemporary plate-glass windows.

FACING PAGE, **Bungalow porches** are conspicuously well built, with their stout pillars, beamed ceilings, and exposed rafter ends. Bungalow porches are high on the wish list of many would-be homeowners.

Along the way, the Bungalow's basic form was influenced by the English Arts and Crafts movement, the Stick style, and the Prairie houses of Frank Lloyd Wright, as well as by Swiss, Japanese, Mediterranean, and Spanish styles. It is difficult to find an architectural expression that the Bungalow hasn't borrowed from or is not compatible with.

MASS MARKETING AND MASS APPEAL

As is often the situation in real estate development booms, architects did not play a major role in shaping these houses. Very few Bungalows were designed by an architect for a particular client or for a particular site. Perhaps for this reason, architectural critics of the time had little respect for the Bungalow as an architectural style.

The Bungalow's lack of legitimacy didn't get in the public's way. Bungalow plans could be purchased easily

With minor changes, the basic Bungalow could be adapted to any number of regional and international styles. Here, the use of ornamental half-timbers in the gable end gives this house a Tudor look.

Marketing the Bungalow

"You can tell the ideals of a nation by its advertisements."   —*Norman Douglas*

BUNGALOWS WERE SHAMELESSLY PROMOTED with advertisements that emphasized the healthfulness of "Bungalow living." Illustrations showed light-filled rooms and suggested the benefits of fresh air flowing through the house, even though Bungalow manufacturers had no control over where their products were assembled. But it was safe to say that many Bungalow owners, having been city apartment dwellers, would find an improvement in terms of light, ventilation, and access to nature.

from pattern books and then constructed by the owner or a local contractor. And for the first time, these homes were mass produced (and mass marketed through mail order) by companies such as Aladdin, Montgomery Wards, and Sears, Roebuck and Co. Manufactured housing was celebrated as a futuristic way to bring home ownership to more people. Families could select a Bungalow style they liked, purchase a complete set of plans, and order all of the building components right down to the paint and finishing nails. Illustrations in the catalogs not only emphasized thrift and ease of construction but also depicted flower gardens and mature trees as romantic symbols of the restorative aspects of home life.

Although the first pattern books referred to Bungalow plans by number, later models had names such as The Calumet, The Champion, The Argo, and The Cadmus. If you live in an older suburb ringing an industrial city, you may be able to walk down the street with a historic plan book in hand and identify the model names of your neighbors' homes.

A Style of Many Flavors

AS AMERICA'S most democratic housing type, the Bungalow has welcomed all cultures and influences, picking up design influences from both North America and around the world. As unlikely as it seems to combine a style that originated in India with flourishes from Switzerland, for example, the mix seems to work.

The Arts and Crafts style was influenced by the British movement of that name, placing value on practical, handcrafted furnishings as an antidote to what was seen as the impersonalization of industrialized society.

Mission-style Bungalows borrowed loosely from Spanish Mission architecture, the colonial style of the Southwest, with its adobe walls and rounded contours. Prairie-influenced Bungalows reflected the design principles of Frank Lloyd Wright's highly publicized homes.

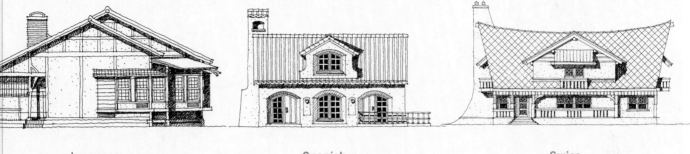

Japanese   Spanish   Swiss

Bungalow Options

Bungalow owners tend to be a faithful bunch, falling in love with their homes and staying put. This explains why Bungalows that come on the market often have had few previous owners and will need to be brought up to date. You might need to consider anything from redecorating to a thorough renovation or major addition. In shopping for our own house, we saw a delightful range of choices within the Bungalow style, most of them relatively unchanged and awaiting the creative ideas of a new occupant. Similar opportunities exist in Bungalow neighborhoods across the country, according to the homeowners and architects we spoke to in writing this book.

We are the third owners of a 1921 Bungalow, and our experience is fairly typical. When we bought it, the kitchen had been updated only once and the improvements were few—the floor and sole countertop had been replaced. The cupboards were original; we were happy to find that the built-in ironing board and spice cabinet were intact. The walls of the one and only bath were adorned with luminescent pink plastic tiles. Although there were two large bedrooms on the second floor, the adjoining attic area was still unfinished and not insulated; frost collected on the heads of roofing nails in the winter. We had found exactly what we were looking for—a small house on a generous lot, within a one-mile walk of our offices. Most critical, it

Traditionally, the hearth has been the center of the home. A fireplace insert is a more cost-effective way to enjoy the beauty of the flames without worrying about expensive heat loss up the chimney.

nonstructural wall ⟶ An interior wall that does not help support the joists in the ceiling above and can be removed without adding structural members to compensate; also, a nonbearing wall.

hadn't been decorated beyond recognition and yet was reasonably maintained.

Remember that, as a housing type, the Bungalow is by its nature adaptable and flexible. Often, the answer to making the house more livable is simply to rearrange the floor plan in the most productive way, without expanding at all. Chapter 2, "Remodeling Inside the Walls," shows interior remodeling projects that do not involve extending the exterior walls or the roof; the chapter includes homes that have been faithfully restored to their original condition. Other options are to raise the roof, add a dormer, find storage space hidden behind existing walls, or build an addition; chapter 3, "Beyond the Walls," covers major and minor additions. Chapter 4, "Brand-New Bungalows," looks at how the style is being interpreted today. The most radical alterations are explored in chapter 5, "The Once and Future Bungalow."

As you will see in the pages that follow, most Bungalow projects are a combination of two or more of these categories. The key to success is thinking clearly in order to achieve a harmonious balance among strategies, from planning right through construction.

INSIDE THE ENVELOPE

Working within a home's existing form is generally the most economical option. Bungalows provide wonderful opportunities to harvest fallow space, particularly second-floor areas under the broad roof. Downstairs, by removing **nonstructural walls,** you can further open up an already unrestricted plan. These steps allow you to gain substantial, useful square footage without reconfiguring either the roof or the exterior walls, at considerably less than the cost of an addition.

The actual expense, of course, will be determined by the extent of your ambitions. Removing a flat ceiling to

The large window, original to the house, brings light into the home on the grayest day of a Seattle winter.

expose the vault of the roof space is relatively economical, but a gut remodel—in which you take the entire house down to its bare structure and basically start over—is more costly. Another variable is how much work you intend to carry out yourself. Redoing a Bungalow is often a labor of love. In the renovation of the Washington State home shown above, the home-owners invested 2,000 hours of their own time.

RESTORATION

There is a great deal of interest in the restoration of Bungalows, as Bungalow societies, web pages, and magazines all attest. If you own a pedigreed Bungalow with lavish woodwork, windows, and detailing, you may choose to restore the home as closely as possible to its original form. Three names come up often in

In keeping with the rest of the house, this kitchen has a serious, almost monumental look, with its banks of dark-stained cabinets and a backsplash of no-nonsense stainless steel.

restoration—two brothers, Charles and Henry Greene, and Gustav Stickley. Greene and Greene were Californians known for their exquisite, elaborate, and expensive use of Arts and Crafts detailing. On the East Coast, Gustav Stickley's straightforward, boldly geometrical furniture is highly sought by Bungalow enthusiasts, and you'll see examples—both antique and currently in production—in homes throughout this book.

If your Bungalow is one of the less richly appointed models, you may want to restrict your restoration efforts to areas that have the most period trappings, usually the living and dining rooms. The other rooms can be left much as they are or be adapted to a more contemporary style.

☆ Wall Treatments

MANY OF US have grown up in rooms with stark white walls, and we don't find the effect to be chilly. But original Bungalow interiors strived to use warm colors and textures to make the home welcoming and cozy. In Craftsman and Prairie Bungalows, wainscoting was a traditional way of ornamenting a plaster wall, but a less expensive option was to cover the walls with burlap or grass cloth. Another popular technique of the period was to apply embossed sheets of paper or linoleum to the walls and ceilings, then paint them to look like plasterwork or tooled leather. All of these

treatments hold up well over the years, with less need for attention than painted plaster or drywall.

To add visual interest and to make interiors look more intimate, walls frequently were given different treatments above and below a picture rail. The horizontal band above this trim might be treated as a frieze, featuring wallpaper, stenciling, or simply a second color of paint. Early Arts and Crafts wallpapers featured hand-printed floral and foliage designs, and manufactured papers made the same look available to thousands of middle-class homeowners. Stenciled

friezes often were geometric versions of natural forms.

Historic sleuthing has shown that original paint colors were more intense and deeper. Today, when lightening your wood stains and selecting your paint scheme, you may want to mute your colors and employ a historic accent color or two.

The clean lines of this new fireplace and mantel show how a Bungalow theme can be updated. The stonework is rugged and is a nice counterweight to the light-hued trim and contemporary furniture.

A wealthy businessman built Bryan and Sandi's Tudor Bungalow in 1923 (see the top photo on the facing page). Their desire was to return this house to its original appearance, and they chose to use traditional Bungalow materials in their renovation. The new walls are plaster, not **drywall,** complete with a picture rail from which to hang their prints. The house isn't strictly a throwback; they gave a nod to new technology (and hot Kentucky summers) by adding central air-conditioning and up-to-date conveniences.

Gary and Beth took a different approach with the restoration of their Seattle Bungalow (see the photo above). Age had prevented the previous owners from keeping up with routine maintenance, and the house was in such rough shape that Gary and Beth had to gut it and re-create its original charm almost from scratch.

drywall Paper-covered panels of plasterlike gypsum. Compared to traditional plaster-on-lath walls, drywall goes up quickly, being nailed or screwed to the wall's studs.

OUTSIDE THE ENVELOPE

We've found that when Bungalow owners add on to their homes, even doubling the size, they tend to take care that the result still looks as though it belongs in the neighborhood. There are various ways of increasing living area without greatly altering the home's modest appearance from the street, and a number of the houses in this book reveal transformations that are almost bafflingly subtle in their effect.

BRAND-NEW BUNGALOWS

When people heard we were writing this book, they often asked us why such a reasonable, attractive style was no longer being built. In fact, Bungalows are under construction across the country. Updated plans are available, and builders in several regions have reintroduced the style to much interest. Architect Thomas Carleton was hired by the community of Spreckels, California, to design several new homes that would be compatible with a neighborhood of historic Bungalows. This was not merely an aesthetic matter of the homes fitting into the existing architectural context; Carleton's designs had to be both affordable and have twice the square footage as the older homes. The identifying marks of a Bungalow are distinctive enough that the style can accommodate both old and new.

☆ Trim Primer

ALTHOUGH A ROOM'S TRIM covers only a small percentage of its wall and ceiling area, the effect can be dramatic. In Prairie homes, the horizontal trim is crucial for tying together the different elements into an architectural whole that is horizontally married to its site. Trim also can take a room back in time or even project it into the future. Here's an inventory of trim commonly used in Bungalows, especially of the Craftsman style, from the floor up.

Baseboard The trim running along the lower edge of the wall, concealing the joint with the floor and protecting the walls. Modern baseboards tend to be simple and narrow; a more traditional look can be had with an intricate profile of two or more milled pieces.

Chair Rail A strip of trim running 2 ft. or 3 ft. above the floor, traditionally used to protect the wall from chair backs. This rail often serves as a border between two different wall treatments.

Wainscoting The paneling on the lower portion of a wall, typically of either vertical beaded boards or frame-and-panel construction. Wainscoting often stops at chair-rail height, but it can be run nearly to the ceiling. It is topped by a cap rail or, if almost the full height of the wall, by a picture rail or a plate rail.

Picture Rail and Plate Rail Strips of trim running roughly 2 ft. below the ceiling. A picture rail is used to anchor wires for hanging pictures and mirrors. A plate rail projects farther from the wall and has a groove to help hold dishes for display.

Crown Molding The trim running along the top edge of a wall, concealing the joint with the ceiling. As with the baseboard, this element can be built up from two or more pieces for visual interest.

ABOVE, **This new California Bungalow** is as bright and breezy-looking as a beach house. The tapered porch columns are an exaggerated quotation from earlier Bungalows and manage to establish the style while defining the house as the new kid on the block.

LEFT, **It's said that newcomers** to California introduced the Bungalow's big roof because it reminded them of rows of rounded street trees back East. That sounds like folklore and yet the appearance of these new Bungalows in Spreckels, California, suggests there might be some truth to the tale.

The built-in cabinets, shiny wood floors, gleaming tiles, and elaborate mantel of this living room show that even in a brand-new Bungalow, the hallmark of beautifully detailed, quality materials carry into the new century.

Changing the Species

WRAPAROUNDS, scrape-offs, and teardowns are dramatic terms that have come about with the heated demand for desirable housing lots. Increasingly, small Capes, Ranches, and Bungalows are purchased only to be torn down to make way for larger homes.

Many communities now realize the need to save older houses from destruction, for a number of reasons. Aesthetically, a big house may dwarf smaller dwellings and cut off the neighbors' sunlight or views. Environmentally, new driveways and bigger roofs can add to runoff and create groundwater problems. Economically, current residents may be forced to sell their homes if expensive new houses create

a substantial increase in tax assessments.

But let's face it. Families do outgrow their Bungalows because some of these houses don't offer much more area than a condo. And some happen to have great sites in great neighborhoods. With the right architect, a radical

overhaul can be sensitively done. It is usually better to do a complete transformation than to tack on an unsympathetic addition. While the exterior may no longer be considered a Bungalow, many of the interior details that people love about their Bungalows can be integrated into the remodeling.

From Duplex to Deluxe

Home buyers with an architectural education seem to find themselves drawn to the Bungalow, both for its pedigree and for its adaptability to bold new ideas. Allyson Nemec, an architect, and Todd Badovski, a remodeling contractor, may have more renovation skills than most Bungalow do-it-yourself couples, but their needs were typical. When newly married, they set out looking for a house that could accommodate a family and found a 1922 home in a rediscovered neighborhood just minutes from Milwaukee's downtown. These are Bungalow streets, characterized by the rhythm of the distinctive low-pitched roofs with their dormers and solid masonry chimneys.

When they first saw the house, it was clad in aluminum siding, but Allyson was immediately attracted to the front porch and the leaded windows. By the time she stepped into the foyer, with its window seat and full closet, she had already decided to make an offer. The attic had been marginally converted into a charmless one-bedroom mother-in-law unit. But downstairs, the formal rooms retained all of the original hallmarks of a classic Bungalow: plaster walls with crown moldings, hardwood floors, built-in bookshelves with **elephant-leg columns** and beveled-glass doors, a mirrored china cabinet, and pendant globe lights.

As a couple who are both professionally and personally interested in historic buildings, they wanted to make architectural changes that would preserve the Bungalow's special qualities while openly bending the usual preservation guidelines. It took several years for their dream to become reality. In the meantime, they lived on the first floor and rented the second-floor apartment to their best friends, who were saving money to buy their own home. The benefit of this slow process

This original door is not energy efficient, nor does it provide much security. But isn't it beautiful? Even if your block is composed of variations of two basic Bungalows, chances are every front door will be different.

elephant-leg columns — Columns often used for Bungalow porches and above the low walls between living room and dining room, so-called because they are squat and tapered.

ABOVE, **Molding, partial walls, posts,** and built-in cabinetry work together in establishing a warm, secure series of rooms.

RIGHT, **From the street,** it is difficult to see that this roof was raised to accommodate two bedrooms, a bath, and a master suite. The owners took great pains to get the angles just right so that their Bungalow would remain in harmony with the neighboring houses.

was that Allyson and Todd got to know both their Bungalow's special qualities and its drawbacks. In the evenings, they would sip the wine they had brought back from their California honeymoon, draw in their sketchbooks, and brainstorm about the house's possibilities within the limits of their finances. The planning process alone took about two years—even architects and contractors have to struggle with hard decisions when a budget is important.

WISHING AND PLANNING

Todd and Allyson's wish list included three bedrooms, one of them a master bedroom with its own bath and walk-in closet; two additional full baths; a family room; a home office, which could double as a fourth bedroom; a small but functional kitchen; and a back porch. They decided to replace the aluminum siding with traditional cedar siding and to reinstall the missing corner boards and other distinctive types of exterior trim. All of this would be accomplished within the original footprint of the home, while removing a number of interior walls and completely altering the roof.

Changes to the existing first-floor plan would not have to be dramatic. The traffic flow worked well, the living room couldn't be more gracious, and the dining room was perfectly suited to family dinners. Bungalows typically have a generous number of windows, often grouped in threes or fours, and the windows on this house both ornamented the exterior and created a delightful play of light throughout the day. The bedroom off the dining room was just the right size for a home office and far enough from the major circulation

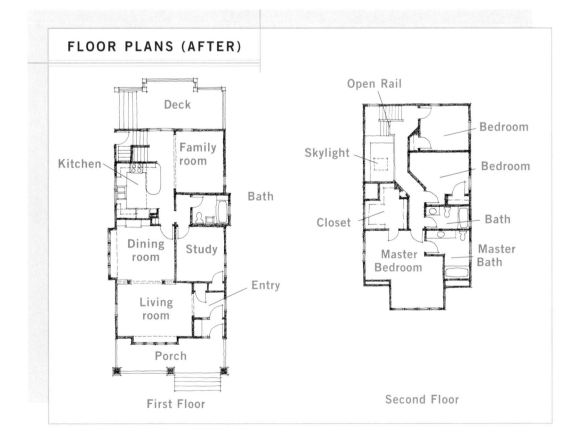

FLOOR PLANS (AFTER)

Deck

Kitchen

Family room

Bath

Dining room

Study

Entry

Living room

Porch

First Floor

Open Rail

Skylight

Closet

Bedroom

Bedroom

Bath

Master Bedroom

Master Bath

Second Floor

ABOVE, **Bungalows are known** for being family friendly, but few original Bungalows were built with a casual family room. Today's owners commonly convert first-floor bedrooms into a family room along with a new kitchen and remodel unfinished attic space into bedrooms.

FACING PAGE, **These custom-made cherry cabinets,** with their leaded-glass doors, are reminiscent of early Bungalow kitchens. Their traditional appearance complements the contemporary light fixtures and the double-height ceiling.

path to provide privacy while remaining within earshot of family activities.

The existing first-floor plan wasn't perfect, however. As is typical in many Bungalows, the stair to the second floor was steep and stuck in a back hallway off the kitchen. The bedrooms were small and plain. The couple envisioned a kitchen that would be suited for both cooking and socializing, although not so comfortable that it discouraged daily use of the living room and dining room. Finally, following Bungalow tradition, they wanted to make outdoor living spaces as accessible as possible.

A FAMILY-FRIENDLY HOUSE

The kitchen hadn't been designed for efficient meal preparation, and all of the appliances and surfaces needed to be updated. Allyson and Todd decided to gut the room—

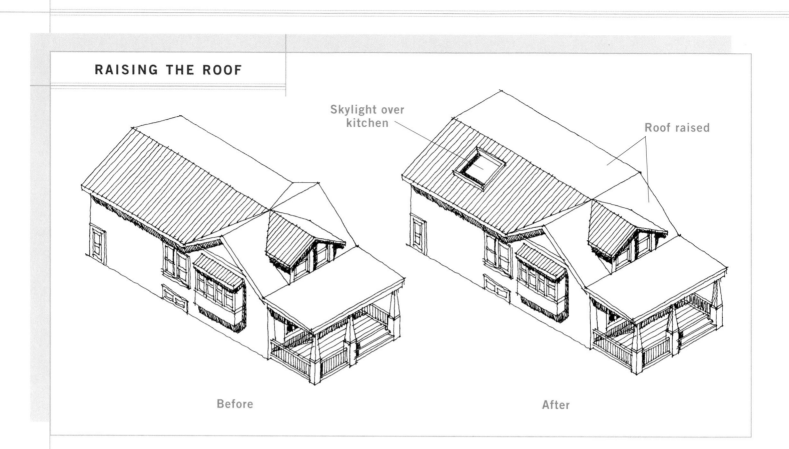

Skylight over kitchen

Roof raised

Before

After

including the ceiling. The new kitchen would be a two-story space that dramatically breaks down barriers, allowing the adults to keep in touch with their children playing up in the second-floor hall. The couple also chose to knock out a bedroom wall to create space for a family room, with a glass door opening onto the back porch. A new handrail helped transform the Cinderella stair into an important design feature. Because the second floor lacked the abundance of detail that made the first floor so inviting, the decision to reconfigure it was not difficult. There was just one nice built-in cupboard on that floor, and Allyson and Todd sold it to neighbors who had the perfect spot for it in their own Bungalow.

Simple design decisions can involve surprisingly complex construction strategies. Even though the goal was to have a modest home, this was an ambitious project. Rather than strictly replicating 1920s' details, Todd and Allyson chose those elements they considered both important and affordable. The new baseboards are 6 in.

high instead of the original 10 in., but they retain the distinctive molding profile. Some of the new woodwork upstairs is painted rather than varnished, allowing the use of a less expensive wood. The new windows have energy-efficient glass, while looking similar to the original **double-hung** units.

SWEAT EQUITY

Allyson and Todd had experience with construction and calculating the related costs, but most homeowners with similar ambitions will find it necessary to hire architects both to envision the end result and to coordinate construction. The renovation took 15 months, with the owners working nights and weekends. The family lived downstairs while they gutted the upstairs, then moved upstairs when the kitchen was gutted. They cooked meals on the Weber grill and washed dishes in the bathtub. While this scenario might not appeal to some couples, Todd and Allyson remember the renovation as a great adventure.

ABOVE, **How do you keep** toddlers out of harm's way—but not out of sight—while cooking a meal? In this Bungalow, a second-floor hall safely overlooks the kitchen below and doubles as a play space.

RIGHT, **Bungalow stairs** to the unfinished attic were strictly utilitarian. When this family converted the second floor to living space, the stair and handrail needed some attention. Red oak was used for the major structure, while wood of lesser quality was chosen for the decorative infill and then painted.

double-hung — A traditional type of window with two independently moving sections (or sashes), one above the other and each held within its own track.

Continuing the Tradition

A casual survey of home magazines will reveal that the great majority of contemporary houses continue to be categorized by traditional styles—Craftsman, Tudor, Queen Anne, Colonial, Cottage, Cape, and Bungalow. People still want to live in homes that convey a sense of community and a connection with the past. The Bungalow, in particular, accommodates a contemporary way of life in a setting that is traditionally crafted of familiar, time-tested materials. It remains one of the most democratic of housing styles, adapting to different regions, personal tastes, and income levels. Trends in housing come and go (consider the once-fashionable sunken living room with its pit fireplace), but the Bungalow has retained respect *and* economic value because of its architectural integrity and fine craftsmanship. Even if previous owners have ripped out trim and tiling and covered the wood floors with carpet, the basic structure of the Bungalow remains as a format within which to restore its charm. And if you aren't a strict traditionalist, a Bungalow can be interpreted in an overtly modern way without compromising its soul.

CONSULT BEFORE YOU COMMIT

As design professionals who happen to live in a Bungalow, the best advice we can give our clients is to forecast how they want to live in the years to come, rather than rush into a renovation project that meets only their immediate needs. To make it a little easier to project into the future, take your architect or licensed home inspector with you when inspecting a house. Even in a frenzied real estate market in which traditional homes are at a premium, the wrong house is still the wrong house.

ABOVE, **To avoid creating a warren** of small rooms in this attic conversion, the architect designed rooms within rooms—with doors that glide and slide for privacy or openness.

FACING PAGE, **Even though the interior** of this Bungalow has preservation status, the landscape is designed for contemporary living.

In more than doubling the square footage of this Bungalow (the original house is to the left), the owners took great care to match the spirit of the style with materials, window design, and a shed dormer.

If you already own a Bungalow, your first stop should be the municipal office, which handles zoning requirements, building codes, and building permits. Look at the local ordinances covering **setback** and height requirements and limits on the percentage of the site that can be built on. How much green space is required? If there is a local design review board, ask about its requirements for submission for review. The point is to make your remodeling plans go as smoothly as possible.

If your project will involve an architect, contractor, or landscape architect, interview several to find one who understands renovation and with whom you feel comfortable. One of the best ways to find a design professional is to knock on the door of a remodeling project you admire and ask the homeowners if they would recommend the people they worked with. Another option is to call the local offices of the builders or contractors association or the American Institute of Architects (AIA) and ask for a referral list. And don't wait until your plans are already gelling. The sooner you bring in a design professional, the better he or she will be able to anticipate your needs. Over and over we hear from our clients that they wished they had brought us into the process earlier, before making big decisions.

Even architects become emotionally involved when buying their own home. We took the precaution of bringing contractors with us when looking at houses. Contractors can help you to make an informed decision—and this may mean throwing cold water on your desire to make an offer.

In many communities, properties are snatched up before a prospective buyer can arrange for a thorough inspection, so it's best to interview and line up your consultants—contractor, architect, inspector—before you go house hunting. This strategy requires a lot more discipline than running out the door when the real estate agent calls and says, "Bring your checkbook," but you will be in command of the process. Once the experts have had their say, you can be confident in making an offer. More than once, we walked away from what we had originally thought was the perfect house. After 17 years in our Bungalow, we have no regrets.

GAZING INTO YOUR FUTURE

If you are already living in your Bungalow, you know why you bought it and have a pretty good idea of what you want it to be. Perhaps you need to put on a major addition because you plan to live in this house forever

Occasionally you come upon a Bungalow that breaks from the norm, as in the stairway of this stone Washington, D.C., home. The elegant spindles are a far cry from those you would find in the typical understated Bungalow stair.

setback ⌒ The minimum distance structures must be from their property lines to ensure a healthy and safe distance between neighboring homes.

ABOVE AND FACING PAGE, **Bungalow tradition dictates** that fine craftsmanship and
quality materials are more important than a
pale imitation of historic details. This new
Bungalow kitchen reflects the way we live
in kitchens today.

and want to comfortably accommodate holiday visits
from friends and extended family. Or you know that
cooking is more important to you than an extra bedroom and want to invest a sizable amount in gutting
and redoing the kitchen. If you expect your job will
require you to move in three years, you might choose
to add a bath or update the kitchen for a higher resale
value. Think carefully about the different stages your
family will go through. The ideal nursery does not
always translate into the perfect teenager's room.
Similarly, it might be tempting to combine the first-
floor bedrooms into one large family room, but if you
have an aging parent it might be best to keep one bedroom with an adjacent bath.

By projecting into the future, you can save time and
money and avoid the inconvenience of redoing a
remodeling project. You may find it easier to finance a
phased construction plan, taking one stage at a time. Of
course, it is difficult in a changeable economy to predict
actual dollar figures. We tell clients to get a grasp on rising costs by tying their budget thinking to the
"Volvo™ Index." For example, a state-of-the-art
kitchen, at any given time, will cost roughly as much as
a new, loaded Volvo station wagon.

Try to be realistic about which tasks you can do
well and which parts are best entrusted to a skilled
craftsperson. A Bungalow's beautiful woodwork may
have to be replaced if you ruin it with a stripping process that gets out of control. Some people are better off
emotionally and financially if they use their hands only
to write checks. Or consider improving your skills; for
example, take a class to learn the correct way to hang
wallpaper. A love of craftsmanship and a sense of thrift
were traits of the original Bungalow owners, and you
can embody them both by getting personally involved
in the renovation of your own home.

CHAPTER TWO

REMODELING INSIDE THE WALLS

ABOVE, **Like earlier Bungalows,** those built in the 1940s were affordable and usually located in appealing neighborhoods. But they tended to be short on charm and craftsmanship, making them perfect candidates for total makeovers.

FACING PAGE, **A key to harmony** in contemporary design is to select one dominant material. In this Bungalow, metallic finishes are used consistently on the major design elements.

MOST REMODELING JOBS TAKE PLACE *inside the envelope.* "Envelope" is a peculiar description for something as substantial as four exterior walls and a roof, but this is the term architects and contractors use to describe the footprint or enclosure of a building. The projects in this chapter look very different from one another—there are raised roofs, new windows and skylights, bumped-up dormers, and rediscovered basements and attics. And yet each stays within the envelope, without the need for an additional foundation.

In most cases, the drama takes place out of sight from the street. There is little outward sign that the floor plans have been extensively reworked in the process of adding and subtracting walls and ceilings. If previous owners stopped by for a visit, they might walk inside and experience the shock of not quite knowing where they were.

Building within the envelope might be the only legal way to expand. In older neighborhoods, where Bungalows are often found, narrow lots and setback

PLANNING ON opening up your Bungalow with new windows, skylights, or a dormer? Your options are numerous but should be carefully considered. Eastern light makes mornings a delight, and southern light provides the greatest amount of light without the afternoon glare of a western exposure. Northern openings take advantage of consistent indirect light—that's why artists favor studios with northern light—but a window or skylight in this elevation will lose heat in colder northern climates. Of course, you may want to bend these rules of thumb to take advantage of a beautifully landscaped backyard or to turn a bedroom balcony into a moon-viewing or sunset-watching pavilion.

requirements often combine to sharply restrict building an addition. In fact, we know of one extreme instance where a permit for a shallow bay window was denied because it would have projected beyond the setback.

So, your one realistic option for expansion may be to rearrange and develop the space you already have. Because of the Bungalow's angular ceilings on the second floor, you may want to consider raising the roof a foot or two to make full use of the area, but even here you may face limitations; be sure to check your community's height restrictions and design guidelines.

If the block you live on is anything like our block of older homes, you won't be alone in your remodeling adventures, and the work on other houses can be an inspiration—especially if you've had a chance to see the interiors before and after the work. On our street, each

morning brings a fleet of carpenters, plumbers, painters, drywallers, masons, air-conditioning installers, and kitchen designers. Scores of vans and trucks make the neighborhood look like a busy scene out of a Richard Scarry children's book.

Rescuing a Home

Reworking an older home is satisfying on a number of levels. The process involves bringing something back—something that was lost, forgotten, or ignored. In speaking with homeowners about the renovation process, we were struck by how many said their homes called out to them, "Rescue me!" Why else would someone buy a house with a crumbling chimney, collapsing porch, rotting window sills, and four ugly layers of roofing?

An older house, if it is to survive, has to capture the imagination of a homeowner. The pivotal feature does not have to be very large or obvious. It can be a stained-glass detail in the built-ins, a glimpse of hardwood floors beneath linoleum, or even a tarnished pendant lamp stashed away in a corner of the basement.

Bungalows have not only built-in cabinetry but also built-in histories. Every owner we've talked to seems to have come upon curious remnants of his or her home's past. Some found old photos and letters tucked into spaces in the walls. In our own Bungalow, we discovered that the subfloor of a closet was made from hand-painted billboards advertising a local paint company. Odder still, when we took down a ceiling, we found seven Heinz™ catsup bottles, each containing one copper penny from the 1920s, balanced on a beam. For our contribution, we placed a time capsule of sorts under a new floor, including what we knew about the history of the house and its previous owners, as well as our family photo and a set of before-and-after plans.

SHOULD YOU RENOVATE?

Most of the projects in this book are carried out in the spirit of renovation: The exterior retains the traditional Bungalow style while changes are made more freely on the inside. The treatment may vary from room to room, keeping close to the original Bungalow intent in some while turning others into another period style altogether. This flexible approach allows you to use relatively inexpensive materials in part of the house, rather than trying to maintain a universally high standard with hardwoods, built-ins, and fancy finish carpentry. This isn't to say that renovating is necessarily inexpensive. The price tag for redoing a kitchen or master bath alone can be as much as adding on a new bedroom.

Still, a change doesn't have be dramatic in order to be significant. Simple and relatively inexpensive alter-

ABOVE LEFT, **Interior glass-block windows** borrow light from the bedroom, lending a sense of spaciousness to the shower stall. As with many remodeled Bungalows, this house does a great job of tucking a bathroom under its sloping roof.

ABOVE RIGHT, **All of the fixtures** in this bathroom are original. If your bathroom has had its charm remodeled away, you may be able to find period fixtures by scouting out estate and rummage sales, antique shops, and architectural salvage shops. Convincing reproductions are only a couple of keystrokes away if you prefer to shop over the Internet.

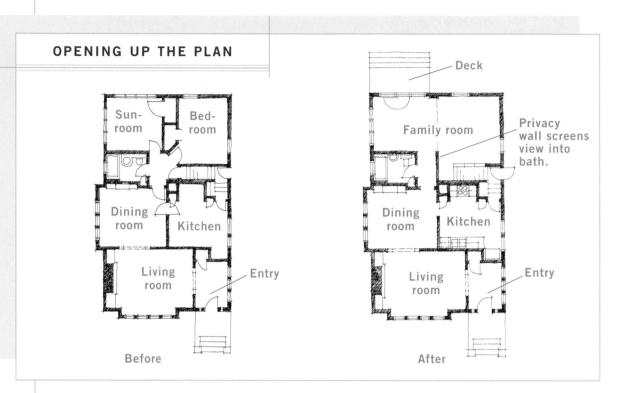

Deck

Family room

Privacy wall screens view into bath.

Sun-room

Bed-room

Dining room

Kitchen

Living room

Entry

Dining room

Kitchen

Living room

Entry

Before

After

This chrome-and-leather kitchen booth is an example of the imprint that Art Deco made on Bungalows in the 1920s.

ations can really change the way you feel about your Bungalow. For example, removing nonstructural walls to open up a room for better views and more light can bring everyday pleasures that aren't calculated in resale dollars. In our own home (see the drawing above), we cut portals into the walls that enclosed the stairway, and now we no longer feel as though we're descending through a dark tunnel each morning. Instead, our first view is of the garden as we come downstairs.

OR SHOULD YOU RESTORE?

A more historically attuned approach is to carry out a restoration, in which you attempt to be as faithful as reasonably possible to the spirit of the period in which the home was built. Because Bungalows typically aren't extravagantly appointed throughout the house, some owners go beyond this stage, choosing to give their homes *more* features of the style than they had when new. Originally, only the public rooms would have been elaborately detailed, but today we tend to want all of our rooms to be brought up to that standard.

Bungalows seem to lend themselves to an eclectic hybridization of architectural styles. In this Historic Register home, the kitchen is classic Art Deco, the living room is pure Arts and Crafts, and the exterior has the effect of exposed timbers that mark the Tudor style.

Restoration is a meticulous process, from the archival research to tracking down original paint colors and authentic door pulls. Luckily for Bungalow owners, there is enough interest in restoration materials that many firms now offer everything from burlap wall coverings to commodes with chain pulls. The costs of a restoration can be considerable even if living space isn't expanded, and this painstaking process often is reserved for buildings of historical significance. You can count on spending more for both materials and the labor of skilled craftspeople.

In the early 1900s, every city had its skilled carpenters, masons, and painters, and even the most humble Bungalow benefited from their abilities. Today, it can be a challenge not only to find the workers but also to enlist them in the sequence you'll need them. Arrange for their services early in the planning process.

The Anatomy of an Attic

A VISIT TO the unfinished second floor of a Bungalow often involves negotiating a narrow stair that ends up in an attic empty except for storage boxes, plumbing vents, and perhaps a historic clothesline.

This level frequently goes uninhabited because of its limitations—the roof is just overhead, and its rafters pitch down to the floor at the house's perimeter. Small windows in gables or dormers typically cast only a dim twilight over much of the area. And until insulation is securely tucked between the rafters, the undeveloped attic is apt to be uncomfortably hot or cold during much of the year.

But there are time-honored ways to make the second floor livable—highly enjoyable, in fact, especially with the help of recent improvements such as central air-conditioning and window coatings that moderate

indoor temperatures. The harvest can be from 30 percent to 70 percent more floor space for your Bungalow, all without pushing beyond the walls.

You can use the lead time profitably to map out each construction step so that crews are able to work in smooth succession.

TURN MAINTENANCE INTO A MISSION

Bungalows seem to change hands infrequently, and if you're shopping for one, you may discover that the home you want to buy has long-overdue repairs. Or, if you're already living in a Bungalow, chances are there is at least one maintenance task that has been put off for years—upgrading the electrical service, putting on a new roof, or replacing old windows with energy-conserving models.

A renovation may give you the opportunity to take care of several humdrum upkeep jobs all at once, in a way that's relatively painless. Brainstorm to come up with a list of both maintenance needs and projects that could make family life more pleasurable. While redoing the roof, for example, you might choose to put in a skylight to illuminate what had been a dangerously dark stairway. If windows have to be replaced, give some thought to making some of them larger than before (while keeping to the traditional style) in order to make more of a great view. Before replacing an outmoded toilet and sink, consider taking the opportunity to clad the lower third of the walls with **beaded-board** wainscoting—a tough job to pull off with these fixtures in place.

Secreted Square Feet

Bungalows are distinguished by that overarching roof, and beneath it lies a wealth of expansion opportunities. In a surprising number of these homes, the second floor is still a largely unimproved attic. It may contain little but storage boxes, a plumbing vent, and a leaning chimney that looks like a prop out of a Hitchcock movie.

A daybed placed along a sloping wall creates an intimate spot that's perfect for cozying up with bedtime stories.

beaded board Boards milled with a decorative bead or "valley and peak" along the edges, used to make wainscoting and cabinets and occasionally for entire walls and ceilings.

Interior "windows" are an inexpensive yet sculptural way to bring light into an interior staircase. These metal rods—really a safety measure—add to the contemporary expression.

knee wall — A low wall built to close off an area under the eaves that is too low for living space but can be used for built-in cabinets and shelving.

The challenge is to turn that triangular volume, defined by the roof framing, into a space with enough headroom to be comfortable (see the sidebar on p. 48).

To many prospective homeowners this raw space is a draw: It gives them the rare chance to design a brand new area in an old house, tailoring it to suit their particular needs and taste. You may be able to coax out enough square footage for a home office, a master bedroom suite, or a den. Because a second floor is typically a private sector of the home, it lends itself to personal expression in a way that the living and dining rooms may not.

OPPORTUNITIES AND CONSTRAINTS

The unusual geometry of a Bungalow's second floor can make furniture layout a bit difficult, with one or more walls in a room at an angle to the floor. You can plan for a **knee wall,** a low vertical wall set in from the perimeter of the house. On the second floor of a Bungalow, a knee wall typically meets the sloped ceiling at a height of roughly 3 ft. or 4 ft. The empty space behind the knee wall is ideal for inserting bookshelves, cabinets, or a chest of drawers. These storage spaces even contribute to the wall's insulation value.

There is a charm to a Bungalow's oddly shaped second-floor rooms. In our own home, this is the closest we adults come to feeling as though we are in a tree house; we enjoy sitting on the floor surrounded by our books and viewing the tops of trees through the skylights, while sunlight and shadows play over the triangulated ceiling planes. A potential side benefit of those slanted walls is that they may mean a room isn't legally a room at all and therefore not taxed as a bedroom. Check to see if your local ordinance states that if more than a certain percentage of a room's walls are sloping, it is exempt from full taxation.

In terms of today's safety requirements, many Bungalows are economically engineered. This is a polite way of forewarning you that the roof, while safe, may be minimal. Consult with design professionals if you wish to alter the roof structure in any way. If you are opening up what had been an inaccessible space, you'll have to add a stair. Or, an existing stair may cry out for improvement if a habitable second floor is to be made more accessible and attractive. If space or clearance is tight, consider putting a dormer or skylight above the stair to provide more headroom and increase the light level in an area where it's especially important.

Bungalow dormers form interesting niches under the ceiling, with a complexity that would be expensive if framed as new construction. A dormer niche is a great place to get down to work. The natural light, the low ceiling, and the defined perimeter all make it an easy place to focus.

Pesky Collar Ties

IN AN UNFINISHED ATTIC, every third or fourth pair of rafters likely will have a horizontal collar tie running between them. In many attics, they are located at the same height as your head and have to be dealt with if this space is to be made livable. They can be replaced, but their function can't be eliminated.

New interior walls, if carefully situated, may do the job of collar ties. A drop ceiling can be used to conceal ties if the ties are relocated somewhat higher on the rafters. Plywood sometimes is applied to the underside of the rafters as a continuous diaphragm that takes the place of the ties. Another alternative is to replace the ties with metal turn rods or cables, leaving them exposed as a high-tech design statement (or as hangers for light fixtures).

Choosing exterior colors for your Bungalow is a decision you will live with for (on average) seven years. Although leaf colors change with the seasons, you can pick one time of year and base your palette on that natural cue. In this house, the paint colors resonate with the carpet of leaves from the yard's silver maples.

ENJOYING EVERY SQUARE INCH

That low roof makes it necessary to lay out the second floor in a certain way. You'll want to center rooms under the highest part of the roof, while placing closets under the eaves to either side. Both beds and bathtubs also can be placed where headroom is less than you need when standing upright. As in any house, a new bathroom is best situated over the kitchen or a first-floor bathroom so that plumbing runs are as short and direct as possible. The vent pipe you see rising up through the unfinished second floor is a tip-off to the plumbing below. Ideally, place bedrooms on the east side of the house to take advantage of the morning light—unless, of course, you are a late riser.

By constructing a built-up insulated roof above the roof **rafters,** leaving them visible from below, you can have an attractive (if rather low) version of a cathedral ceiling. This involves some extra expense because you'll have more ceiling area to drywall and insulate; but the dramatic volumes, interesting light patterns, and maximum headroom may be well worth the cost.

GETTING STARTED

You may want to do some informal polling before deciding on whether to renovate or restore your home. Ask neighbors about their renovating projects—both the pitfalls and the joys. And be sure to ask if the home-owners found that this relatively liberal process erased odd details that make Bungalows endearing. If you're considering restoring your home, ask other Bungalow owners if their restoration project turned out to be too daunting an approach, in terms of expense and difficulty in finding good craftspeople. Jot down the names of architects, contractors, and carpenters who are recommended as having a sense of what Bungalows are all about.

You might expand your outreach to other Bungalow neighborhoods in your area. Local groups such as universities and regional historical societies sometimes have tours of historic neighborhoods, and these events are great opportunities to meet people with similar interests and experiences.

If you are intent on restoring your home, you first have to find out what it looked like when built. Older neighbors may have photographs of the street from an earlier time. You're apt to hear their anecdotes, too, and even if the old stories are more myth than fact, you'll get a verbal picture of your environs as they used to be. Check the local library and historical society for a file of architectural drawings, especially if your home is in a historic district or was designed by a significant architect.

A good bookstore is worth visiting to take advantage of the recent proliferation of titles on the sensitive remodeling and restoration of older houses. Home magazines offer up-to-date information on product sources and Bungalow organizations. There are many other Bungalow owners out there, proud of their renovation and restoration projects and eager to share their tips and experiences. For a list of sources, see p. 198.

A Breezier Bungalow

CROSS-VENTILATION is not the strong suit of a Bungalow's upper floor because the windows typically are restricted to the gable ends, with smaller ones in one or more dormers. There are a few popular solutions to this problem, however.

To get the air moving, you may be able to add another dormer. An operable skylight will have much the same effect, for less money. A traditional answer is to add an operable **transom window** above a bedroom door, where space allows. You also might consider louvered doors or trimming down doors to leave a generous gap (undercut) for air at the bottom. Even if you have central air-conditioning, ceiling fans provide an added benefit because they circulate cool air in the summer as well as warm air in the winter.

rafters — The principal structural framing members of the roof.

transom window — A window placed above a door, often to provide ventilation when the door is closed.

From a Frog to a Prince

ABOVE AND FACING PAGE, **Bungalows often have** an appealingly tactile quality, drawing on rough stucco or smooth river-washed stone or thick wood shingles—real materials from real, identifiable places. One of the delights about this style is that all the houses look as if they have a story to tell—and the setting in which to tell it.

H OW WOULD YOU RESPOND TO A CLASSIFIED AD describing a Bungalow as, "Not for the faint hearted…needs lots of work…classic old-world charmer with potential to be fabulous"?

Gary and Beth jumped at the opportunity to transform this frog of a Bungalow, listed in a Seattle newspaper, back into a prince. As a contractor, Gary was particularly interested in the home's resale potential—the neighborhood's properties were appreciating in value because of their location and their particularly fine craftsmanship. But when Gary showed the house to Beth, she saw more than a real estate investment, and they agreed that this could be their new home. They had been looking for a traditional house that could accommodate their modern lifestyle, and Gary, as both a visionary and a romantic, wasn't discouraged by the fact that the 1912 structure needed a great deal of work.

Taking It Down to the Studs

The rooms were filthy, thanks in part to a major rodent infestation. The smell was so noxious that the house had to be treated with the procedures used to remove odor from fire and smoke damage—it was gutted down to the studs, stripped of all paint, and sprayed with a shellac-based primer.

The Handmade House

ACCORDING TO A CARPENTER who remodeled our Bungalow, the original builder must have had one arm shorter than the other because dimensions are consistently smaller by the same measure left of center. We are reminded on a daily basis that individuals built these older homes.

This is one reason we recommend that you hire craftspeople who have experience with the unpredictability of Bungalows. Old houses settle over time and rarely is anything square. Working on them is similar to learning a foreign language, in that it takes a while to become fluent and to understand the idioms. Even demolition is different in older homes. When we tore away the downstairs walls in our Bungalow, we found just what we expected— wood lath and plasterboard, an early version of drywall. Upstairs, we got a big surprise when the sledgehammer bounced off the wall. After prying the wall open with a crowbar, we found horsehair insulation, wood lath wrapped with wire turkey mesh (larger than chicken wire), and a type of rubble that we still can't identify.

A few happy surprises turned up during the process of deconstructing the house. Twin windows were discovered on either side of the fireplace, where they had been concealed for years within the walls. In the dining room, a dropped acoustic-tile ceiling was torn down to reveal the original beams. It took a worker more than two weeks to strip the paint from the woodwork in the dining room alone, revealing the beautiful grain of the Northwest fir. Fortunately, the plate rail and built-in sideboard were in salvageable shape. Replacements for the damaged woodwork had to be milled on site because the profile (the shape, in cross section) wasn't commercially available. Gradually, the dining room was returned to its original quiet grandeur, with the beams overhead, stained-wood cabinetry and flooring, and the choice of a particularly rich hue of paint.

The **Art Deco** brick fireplace in the living room didn't fit the **Craftsman** image that Gary and Beth wanted. They chose to replace it with one of stone, adding a custom fir mantel. A family portrait hangs above the fireplace with honey-toned fir paneling as a

Art Deco—A style that became popular after the Bungalow appeared, characterized by gracefully streamlined shapes and the decorative use of glass and chrome.

backdrop. Built-in bookshelves were fitted into the spaces on either side of the fireplace, no doubt replacing units that long ago had been removed.

Gary had in mind that the living room would be for daily family use—reading, talking, gathering—and he was careful not to overwhelm the space with too much dark wood. The white trim bounces available natural light into the room. When doing a restoration, restraint is important. Slavish attention to faithful details can give a house a themed look that doesn't feel authentic. Remember, Bungalows were originally built to accommodate the way people actually live, not to impress the neighbors.

ABOVE AND FACING PAGE, **There seem to be two categories** of prospective Bungalow owners. One hopes to walk into a house with a dining room just like the one shown above, with beautiful woodwork, ceiling beams, period lighting, and authentic built-ins. The other would prefer to stumble upon a project like the "before" photo of this same dining room, shown on the facing page, because they prefer a hands-on challenge.

Craftsman ⁓ Another term for the Arts and Crafts movement, which favored a handmade aesthetic with simple materials over mass production.

The kitchen is usually the most challenging room in a renovation because most of us want to have a balance between old and new features. Here, up-to-date appliances nestle into a warm, traditional kitchen with lots of varnished wood, fluted face frames on the base cabinets, warm-hued cork flooring, and pendant lights.

Converting Three Rooms into One

The old kitchen and a mudroom were combined to create a large, new kitchen with a dining booth. The kitchen has the modern conveniences you'd expect to find in a remodeled home, while retaining a quiet, pedigreed look in part due to the care taken with natural materials—a cork-tile floor, wood cabinetry with glass doors, and decorative tile. The windows above the sink look similar to the double-hungs elsewhere in the room, but they are two-paned **casements** that can easily be opened with a crank. The wall cabinets are capped in a way that resembles the window frames, reinforcing the impression that the kitchen needed only minor refurbishing rather than a complete reconstruction. Even the lighting looks convincingly backdated; the suspended lamps resemble old industrial fixtures, with their ribbed-glass domes.

casements — Windows that hinge and open at the side.

ABOVE, **This living room** was gutted down to the studs, leaving the owners free to interpret the room rather than recreate what existed before. A new Arts and Crafts–influenced fireplace replaced the Art Deco original.

LEFT, **Doing household chores** shouldn't mean being isolated in the dreariest parts of the home. Instead of lugging laundry down to the basement, this family located the machines in a large kitchen closet. Cleaning materials are placed on shelves high above a child's reach.

Little breakfast nooks are standard features in many original Bungalow kitchens. This nook combines coziness with efficiency. The seats can be lifted for access to extra-deep storage areas, just right for stowing silver that is used three times a year or coloring books and crayons for a rainy day.

The L shape of the base cabinets creates a nook for the booth. Its high-backed benches have the delicate detailing of an old-fashioned porch or of arbor benches found in gardens in the early 1900s. The table between them is wall supported, and the absence of legs makes it easier to slide in and out of the booth. Lift the uphol-stered seats and there is handy storage space below. The washer and dryer are nearby but kept out of sight behind a trio of five-panel sliding doors.

A new back porch is a couple of steps beyond the booth (see the photo on p. 58). Care was taken to give added importance to its appearance so that it looks far more like an extension of the house than a deck would have. The caps on the posts look like proper hats, and the rails work to form a wooden screen.

Built-up woodwork can have a quietly grand effect, even though the materials aren't particu-larly exotic or expensive. Here, the entry to a bedroom has been trimmed with traditional panels on either side of the passageway and overhead.

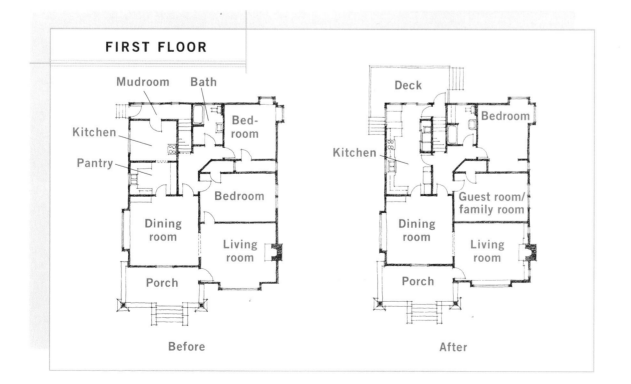

FIRST FLOOR

Before

After

SECOND FLOOR

Home office

Closet

Storage

Master
bath

Master
Bedroom

Storage

Roll-out
storage

Before

After

Neighborhood Relations

A FULL-SCALE REMODELING can be somewhat stress-ful to your next-door neighbors. You can help by tell-ing them about your renovation plans, including when construction trucks will start appearing and when they will disappear. It's also important to talk with your con-tractors before the project begins to let them know what might not be acceptable in your neighborhood—for example, playing loud music, taking up the park-ing spaces along the street, and allowing refuse from the construction site to blow into adjacent yards. Make sure that the demolition dumpster is parked in front of *your* house, not someone else's. You may want to consider renting a portable toilet for the con-struction workers, if allowed by your municipality. And then, when the workers pack up and go away, why not invite the neighbors over to show off your house and thank them for their goodwill?

Harvesting Space

Compared with the appetite for square footage evident in today's homes, Bungalow owners of yesteryear appear to have been on a diet. The original owners of this house lived in less than 900 sq. ft. of finished space. Gary and Beth's plans included creating a master suite on the second floor and converting the basement into a home office. They now have over 3,000 sq. ft. of living space, all within the envelope.

As with the kitchen, the reconfigured second floor looks more like a faithful restoration than brand-new construction. The detailing in the bedrooms is simpler than in the public rooms downstairs. Gary kept the woodwork understated, with a painted finish, but the trim is more involved than you'd find in a typical spec house. Homeowners usually place storage (lots of it) at the top of their wish lists when planning a remodel, and Gary took advantage of the knee walls to carve out bookcases and two rolling linen-storage units that slide out of the wall.

The master bedroom is large enough to accommodate several over-size pieces of furniture, allowing the owners to use this space for cocooning, conversation, and comfort.

Every old house requires maintenance...just to keep up. To reuse these original windows, they had to be removed, stripped, planed, caulked, painted, and reinstalled with modern weatherstripping.

The master bath is a far cry from the strictly functional, antiseptic baths of early Bungalows. Mottled green tiles shimmer under the skylight. The wainscoting is topped by a generous shelf for more storage space. The oversize tub has been placed under an eave with a skylight carved into it.

The landing is flooded with light and fresh air from four casement windows at one **gable end.** The spot was too attractive to treat as a hall, and the couple decided to use the niche for a home office, conveniently placed and yet out of sight from the relaxed environment of the living and dining rooms.

Gary's business office is now in the basement, sparing him a drive to work on many mornings. "It's nice to hear the kids playing in the backyard and great to be able to spend some time with them occasionally during the day," Gary says, "and my commute can't be beat."

Consider the Basement

DEPENDING ON what part of the country you live in, your Bungalow may or may not have a basement waiting to be exploited. Bungalow basements were not designed as additional living space, but then neither were the unfinished attics in many of these homes. If you want to squeeze out more living space from a Bungalow, the basement may be ripe for the plucking. There are several things you should consider, however, before investing any money.

First, how dry is your basement? If you've noticed standing water from rain or melting snow even once a year, we suggest you consider abandoning your plans.

What is the intended use? Basements are particularly suited to a new darkroom, entertainment center, wine cellar, laundry room, or woodworking shop because these will need little if any natural light.

Finally, will it be legal to expand into the basement? Codes may require that there be more than one exit from that level. And if you plan to use the basement as a bedroom or an office, there also may be requirements for window size, even if you aren't discouraged by the possibility that light may be limited.

Don't overlook the potential advantages. Because basements are surrounded by earth, they are relatively easy to heat and shouldn't need cooling in summer. And this new space is relatively inexpensive because any remodeling that doesn't involve a new foundation will cost you less per square foot than an addition.

Sometimes the room itself will give you a clue as to how it wants to turn out. When the chimney was removed from the old furnace in this house, a large hole was created in the roof. Rather than shingle over the area, the owners decided it was the perfect space to locate a skylight, right above the new whirlpool bath.

gable end—A side of the house showing the triangular top story, rather than a pitch of the roof.

A Starter Becomes an "Ender"

ABOVE, **There is more than one surprise** nestled under the roof of this typical Midwestern Bungalow. The unfinished space in the eaves allows the homeowners to carve and sculpt new rooms that express their personal aesthetic.

FACING PAGE, **While talking with their** architect, the owners of this house fondly described their memory of an Italian *pensione* that had a funny little sink right in the middle of the room. This memory inspired the master suite you see here.

S COTT AND LISA JOKE THAT THEIR STARTER HOUSE has become their "ender" because they like the house and the neighborhood too much to consider leaving. They bought this Minneapolis Bungalow before the renewed interest in the style hit the Midwest and drove prices up considerably. At first, their family was small enough to be accommodated nicely without making use of the space on the unfinished second floor. Then, as the kids got older, they needed more room. The couple considered finding a larger house, but the thought of growing in place was far more appealing. They decided to remodel the attic into a master suite.

They worked closely with architect Geoff Warner on the plans and the structural details. Scott's construction experience proved to be a great cost saver. He built walls, designed furniture, installed cabinets, hung drywall, and painted. The only workers brought in were the plumber and electrician, reducing the estimated construction costs by 50 percent. As a result, the couple was able to carry out an ambitious project on a tight budget. And because Scott is a furniture designer by profession, getting involved allowed him to ensure his own high standards for the interior work. Geoff

Interior glass-block windows borrow light from the bedroom, lending a sense of spaciousness to the shower stall. As with many remodeled Bungalows, this house does a great job of tucking a bathroom under its sloping roof.

enjoyed pitching in as well, getting away from the drafting table to do some construction work himself. He and Scott were able to install the skylights on one gorgeous Saturday.

A Sink with a View

The entire second floor was to be just for the parents, and Lisa and Scott went along with Geoff's idea of having one big space that would combine sleeping and bathing areas in a relaxed way. The sink stands in the middle of the room, backed up by an intriguingly shaped wall section that narrows to a column just short of the ceiling. The sink itself is a sculptural conversation piece. By placing it here, the bathroom could be made that much more compact—the same strategy used in small hotel rooms; in fact the couple got the idea from Italian *pensiones*.

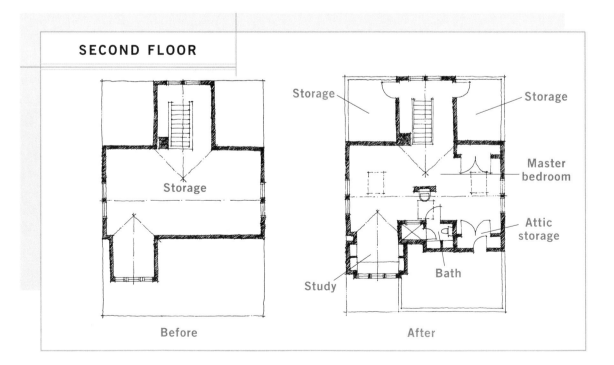

SECOND FLOOR

Storage

Storage

Storage

Master bedroom

Attic storage

Bath

Study

Before

After

The resulting project looks more like an urban loft conversion than a Bungalow bedroom. The minimalist sculptural approach allows each wall surface to be seen as part of a composition that changes as you walk through the space. The skylights, set deep into the ceiling, call attention to that plane as well and help the rooms seem taller than a conventional attic. The effect was largely created with an inexpensive and readily available material—drywall. The exposed brick of the flue and the wood flooring are a visual connection with the older parts of the Bungalow.

A work station for correspondence is tucked under the pyramidal shape of a gable dormer, with two tables and built-in shelves. The light paint colors and blonde

Color, light, and shadows are used effectively as design tools in this attic conversion. The center wall, simply constructed of drywall, is the focal point. As you come upstairs, you're apt to wonder if you are entering a gallery space or a bedroom. The soft blue wall creates an illusion of depth, while the exposed brick of the original flue adds to the loft look.

wood make the small space feel welcoming and cheery—just what you need in a work area where bills have to be paid.

The project was such a success that Scott and Lisa have just finalized plans for a project *outside* the envelope. An enlarged kitchen and a new porch are in their future.

Updated and Upsized

ABOVE, **In the New England countryside,** it's said that good fences make good neighbors. For this Chicago home, with its narrow lot, a glass-block window does the same. The heavy glass allows light to flow into the home while providing privacy from the neighbors.

FACING PAGE, **Although most Bungalow owners** find themselves stripping layers of paint from trim, you may elect to do the opposite: Painting the wood for a lighter effect as was done in this room.

OAK PARK, ILLINOIS, IS KNOWN AS BOTH THE incubator for Frank Lloyd Wright's revolutionary domestic architecture and as a city of highly desirable neighborhoods. Bungalows are ubiquitous. They have a no-nonsense demeanor as they march down the street on lots so tight they could be described as cheek by jowl. The porches weren't designed so much for idly passing the time as for protection from the fierce Canadian winter winds.

Block after block of houses were built to the same setback line, a fact made all the more obvious now that the streets' elms have been lost to disease and the Bungalows are no longer tucked under the overlapping canopy of the majestic trees. Efficiency and affordability were the primary assets of these Bungalows. But on the inside, the beautiful woodwork and artful leaded glass are especially gracious, making each home special and different from its neighbors.

Because Frank and Jo's lot is so tight, adding on outside the envelope was not an option when the previous owners asked architect David Seglin to expand their living area. The only places to go were down into the basement and up into the unfinished attic. In the process, David transformed 2,800 sq. ft. of unused space, substantially adding to the home's original 1,600 sq. ft.

ABOVE, **This house was one** of 90,000 Bungalows recognized when Chicago celebrated the Year of the Bungalow in 2001. Recognition is in order because from the street these modest homes barely hint at the wealth of detail and spaciousness within.

FACING PAGE (LEFT), **One of the intentions** of the new owners was to integrate the dining room more fully into the rest of the floor plan. Removing walls opened up the room, and adding columns reinforced a sense of formality.

Popping the Top

David is an outspoken critic of Bungalows. He thinks they are archaic—the rooms too small and the bathrooms too few—so that the houses aren't suited for today's lifestyles. But he does acknowledge that they have terrific potential for remodeling with all of their untapped area. This Bungalow originally had three small, cramped bedrooms on the first floor. To ensure that the new second floor would be spacious, David convinced the owners to go to the expense of lifting the roof. This would make the entire area of that floor fully habitable, including the perimeter that otherwise would disappear behind knee walls. So it was that the second floor, once devoted only to storage, blossomed into a master suite with a walk-in closet and a generous bathroom, plus two other bedrooms with a shared bath.

Bungalows usually have one or more dormers illuminating the second floor. In this home, David created a lightwell using the existing dormer to bounce light down into the dining area. This room has a number of highly ornamented windows, but the closeness of the neighboring house blocked just enough natural light that a creative solution was needed to enhance the dining experience.

Light is harnessed in an innovative way in the kitchen as well, and again the challenge was dealing with the proximity of the house next door. A large window was redone with glass block so that this large area shimmers with light while creating a sleek cloak of privacy. If the couple chooses to eat breakfast in their bathrobes, the neighbors are none the wiser.

Skylights for Subtlety

☆ **SKYLIGHTS** are especially suited to the second floor of a Bungalow, with its low roof and the need to make the most of light and ventilation. These windows in the roof can turn what was unusable or unappealing space into prime real estate, for considerably less than the cost of a dormer. What's more, a skylight, with its low profile, will be compatible with the lines of your house, so that it is unobtrusive or even invisible from the street.

Cutting an opening into a roof is serious business, of course—typically, a portion of one or more rafters is removed—and you should consult with an architect or engineer. With careful planning and preparation, a skylight can be installed in as little as a day.

The light cove in the ceiling radiates light from the original dormer above.

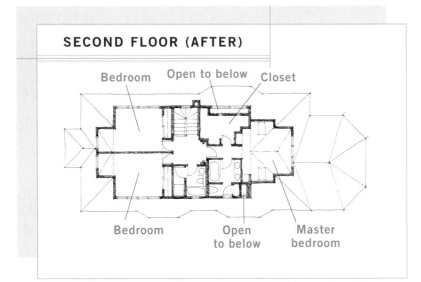

SECOND FLOOR (AFTER)

Bedroom · Open to below · Closet

Bedroom · Open to below · Master bedroom

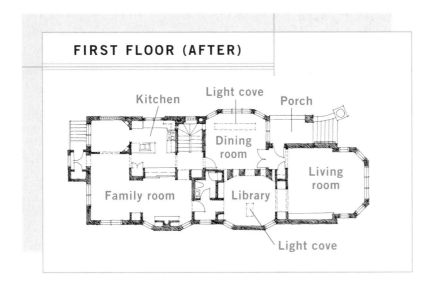

FIRST FLOOR (AFTER)

Kitchen · Light cove · Porch

Dining room

Living room

Family room · Library

Light cove

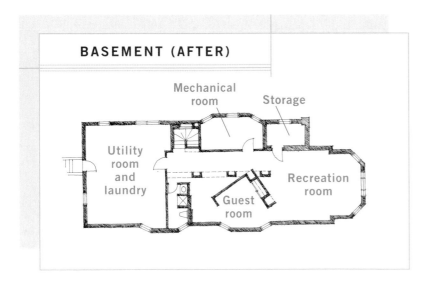

BASEMENT (AFTER)

Mechanical room · Storage

Utility room and laundry

Guest room

Recreation room

An Open Plan

Reducing visual clutter was a major goal of the remodeling. David suggested doing away with all the first-floor walls that could be removed without compromising the structure. The result is a series of framed views and flowing spaces. In the process, he reduced a total of ten doors down to just three—a sure sign that a floor plan has been opened up significantly.

Two outstanding features of this house—the woodwork and windows—needed little help to look their best. The woodwork was particularly fine, although many of the baseboards had been covered up by cumbersome cast-iron radiators. Electrical and zoned forced-air heating and cooling allowed the removal of these distractions. And in response to the long gray winters in Chicago, both the formal rooms were graced with an abundant number of windows—not just any windows but casements with a lavish amount of leaded art glass and topped by arched clerestories for even more light. The faceted glass refracts color and light onto the walls and ceilings, celebrating every last ray of sunshine on a winter afternoon.

The original living room fireplace was built from dark brown brick in a busy pattern, and Frank and Jo asked that it be redone in a way that wouldn't be a distraction from the extraordinary windows. David faced the fireplace with white-streaked green marble for a contemporary note in an otherwise strictly traditional room.

The kitchen and family room are altogether more modern. The whimsical patterning of the cream, black, and tan tiles pays tongue-in-cheek homage to the tradition of Bungalow tilework. The white cabinets have red accents that pick up on the red glass used in the windows of the formal rooms. The woodwork here is painted in

ABOVE LEFT, **The glossy finish of this oak floor,** sometimes referred to as a basketball-court finish, may be just what you're looking for, but there also are products that give a moderate or low luster. Before having a floor refinished, look into the newer techniques that are more environmentally friendly than previous methods.

ABOVE RIGHT, **Using such simple materials** as drywall, baseboards, and paint, as well as the design principles of rhythm and repetition, the entrance into the master suite is heralded as a major event. This doorway echoes the multiple sets of doors on the first floor.

ABOVE, **Bungalows can be difficult** to pin down to one specific architectural style. This pleasant ambiguity allows a Bungalow to accommodate a wide range of furnishings, from antique to modern. To make a room better suited to contemporary furniture, you can use brighter colors than the quiet terra-cotta, browns, beiges, and viridian green of early Bungalows.

FACING PAGE, **The streamlined kitchen,** with its sleek surfaces, is designed to contrast with the home's authentic Bungalow details.

white and soft grays for a more contemporary look than would be had with stained and varnished wood.

Frank and Jo's home manages to bring together both traditional and modern elements without discord because care was taken to blend at least a bit of both in each room. The front rooms are very much in the Bungalow period, but the furniture is contemporary—and there's that striking lightwell over the dining table.

The kitchen looks completely modern at first, until you notice the quiet touches at foot level. The floors are wood, and the baseboards have the built-up look of vintage trim, which was made of several pieces for a more complex profile. That's all it takes to make new rooms look as though they belong to the Bungalow.

Including the Kitchen Sink

If you can't have the butler, a butler's pantry—with an extra sink, second dishwasher, and added counter space—goes a long way toward making entertaining more fun. An old window was replaced by stained glass, lit from above like a painting.

THE KITCHEN IS THE ONE ROOM IN A HOUSE that tends to be renovated with each change of owners. No doubt that's because most of us are particular about both the mechanics and the look of our kitchens. Mary Ann thought her 1908 Chicago Bungalow was lovely and livable—except for its kitchen. The kitchen was small and dark; its view was of the side of the house next door—all of 6 ft. away; and it was located in the middle of the house, far from the garage, so that bringing in groceries was more than the usual inconvenience. Another flaw of the original plan was that there was no easy access to the small but attractive backyard, discouraging the family from dining outdoors.

Mary Ann felt strongly that the remodeling shouldn't sacrifice links with the past in favor of functionality. She chose Chicago architects Greene and Proppe because of their experience renovating homes from the early 1900s. This team reworked the floor plan to turn the old kitchen into a butler's pantry, while creating the new kitchen from the good-size mudroom and family room. The back porch was rebuilt, providing convenient access to the kitchen and family room. Most important, the

Prior to the remodeling, the back of the house was chewed up into a warren of small rooms that had no connection to one another. While early Bungalows stressed family togetherness in the living and dining rooms, it was everyone for him- or herself in the other rooms. Today, most Bungalow renovations include a family area. The quality of construction in this family room rivals the look and feel of early Bungalow rooms, but it is far more relaxed.

The owners of this house requested that their new kitchen have a strong connection to the property. Transom lights, casement windows, and a glass door visually link the kitchen to the porch. Outside, windows in the lattice link the porch to the yard.

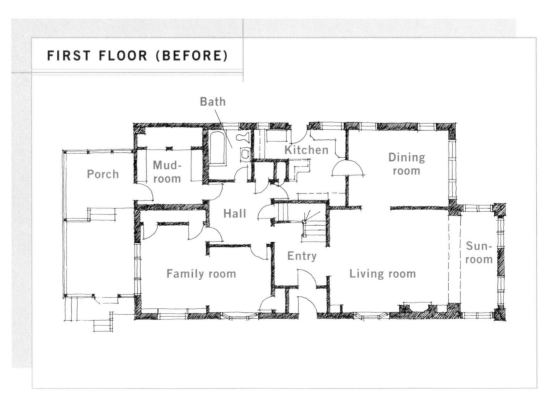

FIRST FLOOR (BEFORE)

Bath

Porch

Mud-room

Kitchen

Dining room

Hall

Family room

Entry

Living room

Sun-room

family finally has a direct connection to the yard, fulfilling a Bungalow hallmark.

A New Old Kitchen

Cupboards tend to set the tone of a kitchen, and the model Mary Ann chose looks more like oak cabinetry than kitchen fixtures, with traditional styling, pulls, and stone countertops. This, along with the wood flooring, helps the room to feel like an integral part of the house.

As with Frank and Jo's house discussed on pp. 70–77, glass block is used because it admits a flood of light while creating privacy. In a novel approach, the glass-door cupboards are mounted so they appear to float a couple of feet in front of this glass wall. The contents—mostly glassware—are set aglow, with an effect something like the warm, multicolored view through a stained-glass window. Good lighting is crucial in a

Chicago summers can be hot, muggy, and buggy, making this wood ceiling fan more than an attractive accessory. The porch looks like a garden room—with the trellis, its articulated caps on the vertical supports, and the beaded-board wall. These are not standard details. The porch has been brought up to the level of thoughtfulness and quality of the rooms inside.

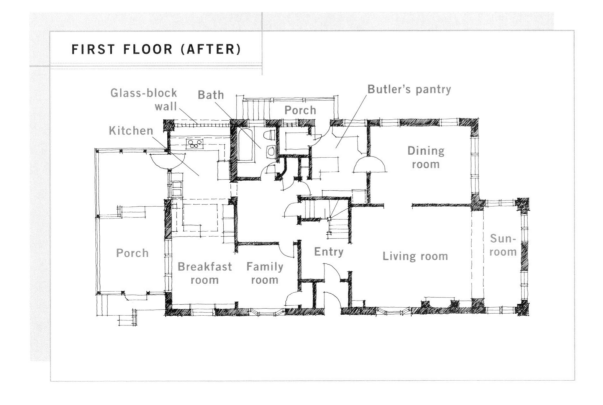

FIRST FLOOR (AFTER)

Glass-block wall · Bath · Porch · Butler's pantry · Kitchen · Dining room · Porch · Breakfast room · Family room · Entry · Living room · Sun-room

Coved ceilings usually are reserved for dining and living rooms. Because this room is often used for parties, special features like this one add to the enjoyment.

Keeping Up with an 80-Year-Old Kitchen

TODAY'S KITCHEN DESIGNERS call for more and larger appliances, fancier fittings, and space-age surfaces—and the average kitchen is remodeled every 7½ years. Why not aim for a kitchen remodel that lasts at least twice as long as the national average? The best way to do that is to put in a kitchen that is relatively true to an enduring period style.

If you are fortunate enough to have a kitchen that has not been repeatedly remodeled, take a good look at what it may have to offer. Original base and wall cabinets are better constructed than many newer models and may be transformed simply by refinishing or, at greater expense, by replacing the doors and face frames. Even refinishing tarnished pulls can help make a kitchen come alive.

Utility was the main idea behind original Bungalow kitchens, drawing on a limited palette of wood, tile, and stone for their durability, natural beauty, and ease in cleaning. These materials do not lose their looks as they age, nor do they tend to go out of style. Another timeless aspect of the Bungalow kitchen is storage that is well thought out. Foldaway ironing boards, linen drawers, and built-in iceboxes were once the norm; you can plan for niches in which to incorporate such modern-day items as recycling bins and microwaves.

kitchen for ambience and efficiency. Four types have been employed here—under-cabinet lighting, recessed can fixtures, up-lighting, and decorative pendant lights. The cupboards are backlit at night, so they continue to be an attention-getting feature after the sun has set.

And how did the old kitchen fare in its transformation into a butler's pantry? Located off the formal rooms, it has a second dishwasher, second oven, double sink, and still more counter and storage space, making it a great staging area for food prep and cleanup when entertaining. The black-and-white floor tile, beaded-board wainscoting, and plate rail pay homage to Bungalow kitchens of the past.

Porches Can Have Windows, Too

Privacy is at a premium in Chicago's urban neighborhoods, and the corner location of Mary Ann's house was too open to view for comfort. The new porch uses a trellis for a semitransparent wall that allows light and air to pass through. Trellises are appropriate to the period and are enjoying renewed popularity in garden architecture. This one was cleverly made with cutouts that act as windows, so that the family can still be part of the neighborhood while enjoying the sense of enclosure of an outdoor room. The rebuilt porch also has plenty of flexible seating that can double as tabletops for large parties or as plant stands when only the family is present. The cedar ceiling is similar in tone to the trim in the kitchen, helping to visually connect the two spaces.

CHAPTER THREE

BEYOND THE WALLS

ABOVE, **Outdoor rooms** deserve the same attention to material selection and detailing that indoor rooms do. After all, they are the introduction to your home.

FACING PAGE, **The new addition,** on the right, more than doubled the square footage of the original Bungalow. By stepping the addition back, the integrity of the original Bungalow is still evident.

E VEN IF YOU CLEVERLY EXPLOIT EVERY NOOK AND cranny of your Bungalow, the house may still be too small for your family's lifestyle. When you come to this point, it's time to step back from the house and consider an addition—building *outside the envelope.*

A few challenges may be immediately obvious. First, there is the Bungalow roof. Because of its distinctive pitch and mass, this style is not the easiest to add on to. For example, how do you connect an addition and integrate the roof forms? Then there is the Bungalow's modest, ground-hugging nature. Will the addition over-whelm the original house? How vertical can it be and still fit in? Can you add a true second story and be faithful to the Bungalow style? As the examples in this chapter make clear, a carefully thought out addition can reinforce the proportions and timeless qualities of a Bungalow, while giving you all the space you need.

ABOVE AND RIGHT, **Outdoor living** is a Bungalow hallmark, as is its regionally distinctive design. This Midwestern Bungalow incorporates a screened-in porch, necessary to enjoy the out of doors without inviting insects in.

Why Add On?

There may be several reasons to add on. While Bungalows are often perceived as starter homes, their buyers tend to find that they like both the house and the neighborhood so much that they are reluctant to move and so choose to stay. Another factor is that putting an addition on a Bungalow is usually less costly than trading up to a four-bedroom Colonial house on the same block. That said, keep in mind that an addition outside the envelope is not going to be an inexpensive option. If you bought a Bungalow a couple of decades ago, when they were relative bargains, the price tag of a master suite addition and a kitchen remodel may easily equal the original purchase price.

IS AN ADDITION REALLY NECESSARY?

As you refine plans for an addition, you're apt to wonder at some point if you really need to go to all that expense. Your architect may prompt these doubts by questioning if the addition has to be so big or by suggesting that building a new foundation for a 4-ft. bump-out just isn't worth the expense. Even if your design professional doesn't challenge you on this, we suggest you examine your own assumptions about how much space you need. The answer may not be *more* square feet but *better* square feet. (If you find this to be the case, see chapter 2.)

We once had clients who insisted they needed to double the square footage of their house, including a fourth bedroom, a larger dining room, a family room, a home office, and a three-car garage. We discovered that they already had sufficient space, but that it was largely unusable because it was the most cluttered house we had ever seen—a difficult point to broach. In carefully

Floor-to-ceiling windows bring the outdoors into this Bungalow.

chosen words, we convinced the couple that making their home twice as large might only double their problems. Our new design, which reconfigured many of the existing rooms, allowed them to get the additional function they needed with an addition half the size they anticipated.

Homeowners often are too close to their house to see its positive aspects—they think that if only they had more room, all their problems would disappear. We encourage you to look at the existing plan to see what is working now and what isn't; otherwise, adding on may do away with desirable features that had been a quiet comfort or a subtle pleasure.

For many families, children are the spark plugs that ignite bold thoughts of an addition. When the parents finally launch into an expansion that has been on the

A contrast of old and new is evident throughout this house. The glass pendant lamp calls attention to the cove molding, evocative of an earlier era, and contemporary art glass is displayed in the traditional built-in cabinet.

drawing board (and computer screen) for years, their enthusiasm may be dampened by the thought that the kids soon will grow up and leave. But the need for space won't necessarily be diminished. When grown children return to visit, they usually don't come alone. Early on, they bring college friends home, and eventually they show up with families of their own. And increasingly, if their parents live in a desirable city, the kids move right back into their childhood bedrooms—the rent and convenience are hard to beat.

Americans continue to reinvent the definition of family and, today, three generations living under one roof is no longer an oddity. We have found that in planning an intergenerational house, privacy is a key to harmony. It's often up to the owners, as members of the "sandwich generation," to expand the living area to allow the right mix of social spaces and away spaces.

A growing number of family members isn't the only reason to add on, of course. It may be that you want a home studio or office, more room to entertain, or more wall space to display a collection.

There also could be a financial incentive to expand, and this is something to keep in mind when shopping for a house. As real estate values escalate, you may find that the lot is more valuable than the house itself. That, in turn, can make it difficult to get a mortgage on a 900-sq.-ft. house. But if you apply for a loan with a proposal to add on, you may have a better chance of getting financing—and you'll end up with a house that has enough space.

Until recently, most urban Bungalow neighborhoods were protected from the rash of teardowns because the lots are too tight to accommodate the big houses that typically spring up on cleared property. It might take two Bungalow lots to provide enough space. But recently, long, skinny, tall "sliver" homes have been showing up in architectural magazines as an answer for narrow lots in the desirable neighborhoods where Bungalows are often found. A more resourceful answer is to work skillfully with the existing house, making it roomier while maintaining its character, at least from the street.

Why Not Add On?

Americans like space and lots of it. More than two centuries of design history have shown that. The Bungalow's homey image may make it difficult to conceive of these houses undergoing a bold, sweeping expansion project. But if you want a big house, even a really big house, there is no reason why it can't be a Bungalow. You can add hundreds of square feet and still be true to the Bungalow hallmarks and scale, as the homes in this chapter demonstrate.

In fact, when care is taken with design and material selection, the addition may end up looking older than the original, so that a passerby wouldn't even guess that the existing house was added onto. We've found that most Bungalow owners add on in a sensitive way, no doubt because they were initially drawn to the style at least in part by the visual harmony along the street that is created by a congregation of Bungalow elevations.

COMPOSE A LOVE LETTER TO YOUR HOME

To get off to a good start, identify the things you value about your Bungalow (or the Bungalow you might buy). Try writing what we call a love letter to the place where you live. For example, sunlight may flood the first floor in a way that lifts your spirits every morning. That, in turn, could suggest that it would be worth the extra expense to buy more windows or even to order

Exposed knee braces are a common Bungalow feature. By altering the scale of this and other trademarks of the style, new work can be made to look contemporary while being consistent with the original details.

Take the Plunge

THE FIRST TOUGH DECISION in planning a major renovation is whether or not you should go through with it. The local real estate market may influence your decision. If it is booming and you plan on selling in the not-too-distant future, chances are better that you will get a decent return on your investment. Otherwise, you may be more comfortable taking a number of baby steps over a period of time. In talking with clients, we differentiate between the short-term investment in a "house" and the long-term, phased investment in your "home."

special leaded or stained-glass units to take full advantage of the sunny exposure.

Involve your entire family in this letter—you might be surprised by their responses, calling out rooms or details that you hadn't considered. Your daughter might love a space where she can cozy up with a book on a winter's day. Your son might comment that he has always liked the contrast of dark varnished wood against light-colored walls.

The list will make it more likely that you'll preserve the elements that attracted you to the house in the first place, as well as subtleties you have come to love over time. This description will set a quality standard for the new space so that you don't merely focus on gaining square footage. Also, you'll be better able to express your desires to a design professional. Homeowners tend to be shy about making their ideas known, but this is exactly what good architects want to hear. Their job is to translate your hopes, dreams, and needs into physical form.

Finally, the family's list of positive qualities may suggest which design approach the addition should take. You will see interpretations in this book that cover the

gamut from strictly traditional to contemporary to hybrids of two styles—all in an unapologetic way. Don't be surprised if your ideas change when you go through preliminary discussions with your design professional. As you learn more about Bungalows, you may lean toward being faithful to period design. Or you may start out as a traditionalist, like Nannette and Charles, whose home appears later in this chapter, and enjoy (as they did) that your Bungalow begins to take on a new character once the addition is framed out. As the project went along, this couple felt freer to make changes in a contemporary spirit, without compromising the qualities they admired in the classic Bungalow.

FACING PAGE, **This breakfast room** feels something like a porch, with its side-by-side double-hung windows. The use of a smaller upper sash allows an uninterrupted view through the lower pane.

RIGHT, **Gracious outdoor living** is a hallmark of Bungalows and Texas hospitality. The new balcony follows the geometry of the deck, which was an earlier project.

ABOVE, **The new gables** on the back of this Washington, D.C., Bungalow are repeats of the double gables seen from the street. In the front, they are merely decorative; in the back, they provide much needed headroom for two new rooms.

FACING PAGE, **Double trim pieces** spring from the beam and add interest to the vaulted ceiling of this Iowa Bungalow.

REMAKING A BUNGALOW IN YOUR STYLE

Most of the homes in this book are free adaptations, retaining the hallmarks of the Bungalow while breathing new life into these structures so that they should function well for another 100 years. Adding modern conveniences—air-conditioning, new heating systems, recessed lighting, and low-maintenance appliances—may require some architectural compromises. But these are homes, after all, not museums, and they should express who the occupants are. (Only one of the houses featured in this book is on the National Register of Historic Places, and even it has a patio that reflects the owners' contemporary lifestyle.) "Eclectic" is a word that often crops up when we ask homeowners to describe their design philosophy. Their approach is that Bungalows were designed for relaxed family living and not to impress the neighbors.

Matching the quality of early 20th-century craftsmanship can be difficult. As an example, most original Bungalows had plaster walls, and good plasterers are scarce these days—not to mention expensive to hire. In this case, drywall is the common substitute, and although it is typically used in conventional ways, the sheets offer sculptural possibilities if handled imaginatively. They can follow the lines of the Bungalow roof to the ridge, with a dramatic intersection of angles. And if bent into bold shapes, they add to the traditional Bungalow vocabulary of forms.

Contemporary construction rarely uses the elaborate wood moldings that had been the standard in earlier homes, and you may want to ensure that your vintage baseboards and crown molding don't disappear in the process of renovation. A simple solution is to carefully remove the trim and even floor boards from an area that will be gutted, then refinish them for use in new rooms. If you'll need more woodwork, you might visit

Choosing the right finish is critical when the woodwork is elaborate. The light finish on this newel post allows the beauty of the grain to shine through.

architectural salvage warehouses, check for building materials in local classified ads, or ask friends, architects, and contractors if they know of remodeling projects that aren't reusing the molding, built-ins, or flooring.

It may help to think of trim elements as furnishings. In this way, you'll be more likely to consider their contribution to the interior as you make your plans. Install the high-quality decorative moldings where they will be seen to best advantage, as was commonly done in original Bungalows. Elsewhere, you may choose to get by with painted moldings of lesser quality; they can be as attractive as the high-quality moldings if the paint colors are chosen carefully. For example, if you plan on furnishing the living room with large pieces that will conceal much of the baseboard, you may be able to get by with using less-expensive trim there.

Sometimes, just a reminder of the earlier Bungalow era is enough to make a new room seem a part of the original house. By going overboard on period lighting or heavily carved wood, it's possible to run the risk of taking a house back to the earlier Victorian era, when effects were often overbearing.

☆ Finessing a Floor

bungalow style

IF YOU REMOVE a wall in the process of remodeling, you'll probably be faced with an unlovely strip without flooring. The problem is complicated when the flooring to either side of the wall was installed in different directions or with different materials. The more conservative fix is to make the transition with a patch of flooring that matches one direction, while running flush with the other. Another is to accentuate this difference with a contrasting material or color; this patch will have to be large enough to look intentional, rather than appear like an oversight. And borrowing from medieval Japanese construction, we patched our floor in such a way that we can always hear our kids return from a late night out!

Good craftspeople—tile setters, finish carpenters, and glass artists—can be as important for ornamenting new Bungalow rooms as they once were for the original rooms.

THE UPWARDLY MOBILE
KITCHEN, BEDROOM, AND BATH

In original Bungalows, there was a hierarchy between the richly detailed public part of the house and the somewhat utilitarian bedrooms, bath, and kitchen. Since then, the floor plan of the American home has evolved so that these underplayed rooms are no longer second fiddle. Perhaps most dramatically, the kitchen has replaced the fireplace as the center of our homes; family and friends prefer gathering there than in the dining room or a formal living room. The original Bungalow kitchen, with its emphasis on utility, could never have accommodated all the kibitzers and sous-chefs who want to get involved at mealtime.

Bedrooms originally were not thought of as anything other than a place to sleep and store clothing. Bathrooms were small, spartan, and hygienic, and one per Bungalow was sufficient. Today, the norm is to have a master suite with its own bath, and a large bath for the rest of the family. Even though twin sinks, twin showerheads, skylit whirlpool tubs, and heated towel racks may be standard fare, you can quote earlier traditions—tile, woodwork, pedestal sinks—to make sure the new bathrooms fit comfortably in your Bungalow.

Windows also followed the Bungalow hierarchy, with particularly interesting ones used in the living and dining rooms. When you plan an addition, choosing the appropriate windows will be one of the most important (and potentially one of the most expensive) decisions

This new master suite addition has a balcony instead of an old Bungalow tradition, the sleeping porch. The glass door to the balcony makes the room appear even larger than it is.

Tile Tales

AN ORIGINAL TILE FLOOR speaks volumes about the concern for quality materials, cleanliness, and efficiency. Whether you want to repair, replace, or replicate that tile floor, it's important to know what's going on beneath the surface. The tile was most probably set in a bed of mortar on a concrete pad reinforced with metal lath, all of this on a subfloor. The weight was supported by floor joists spaced more closely together than usual, and the floor was probably lowered or trimmed to accommodate this additional material depth. Removing the tile and putting in another material may be harder than patching it. You can also apply a new tile floor over the old one. Today's construction has been streamlined to greatly reduce the bulk, depth, and complexity of the setting bed.

you will make. Take your cues from the existing windows to ensure that the new units are in the same spirit, without necessarily being identical. For example, if the originals have an upper sash with three panes over a lower sash with one pane, you can use this three-over-one pattern in selecting windows in a variety of sizes or shapes.

MAKE THE MOST OF YOUR YARD

When considering an addition, you also have a chance to address any shortcomings your lot may have. The grade may be unsuited to outdoor activities, for example. And a home landscape changes over the years—sunny gardens become shade gardens as trees mature and what was once the prime place for a swing set is now the herb garden. Across the country, Dutch elm disease wiped out the giant elms that created shady bowers over Bungalow homes. Small pines planted by a previous owner may tower over the house, and the scale may no longer be correct.

Walk around your yard and consider the views, sunlight, and ambient breezes. Depending on how it is sited, an addition can help you get more enjoyment out of your property's best features while screening views of neighbors, traffic noise, and the heat of the afternoon sun. If grading and retaining walls will be part of the plan, be sure to budget for the added expense.

One of our pet peeves is the design amnesia that afflicts many homeowners when considering a new porch or deck. Somehow, they forget about consistency of style and appreciation for detail when planning these outside living areas. For inspiration, look at the examples in this chapter. From a traditional veranda to a contemporary deck, these additions fit in so well that they look as though they could be another Bungalow hallmark.

A series of oversize double-hung windows captures the views to the large yard. The divided-light upper sashes tie these new windows with the originals in the older part of the house.

☆ Porches and Decks for Gracious Living

NOW THAT THE SUBURBAN DECK has become a ubiquitous sight, the front porch is again finding favor with homeowners. An inset front porch is a major hallmark of the Bungalow, of course, and it is the perfect place to hang out for homeowners who want to present an open, friendly face to the neighborhood. By adding another porch to the south or west elevation, you can help shade the house from the summer sun. A new porch also can make the Bungalow's plan more spacious.

For a new porch to fit in well with a Bungalow, its roof should spring from an existing roof or line of the home and be built at the same or similar pitch. And don't rule out a deck, which remains especially appropriate for the private and casual family events typically held in the backyard. It will fit in with the house better if it is aligned with the first-floor elevation and trimmed with elements of the home's detailing.

A Home with a Hearth

This Bungalow is unusual in that it has twin gables flanking its entry, for a composed and balanced appearance from the street. There is little clue that an ambitious two-story addition has been added to the back, dramatically enlarging the home.

load-bearing walls ⌒ Interior walls that support the ceiling joists or roof rafters running overhead. Unlike non-bearing walls, they cannot be removed without providing another means of holding up the structure.

OCCASIONALLY, A SINGLE FEATURE WILL CATCH the eye of prospective homebuyers and clinch the sale. When Tom and Bill saw the massive stone fireplace in this Washington, D.C., Bungalow, they knew it was the house for them. This was a good match—the home needed owners with enough vision and energy to breathe new life into the tired and faded interior. They set about making sure they could view the fireplace from other rooms on the first floor. This goal alone was a major step, as it meant removing **load-bearing walls** and replacing them with columns.

The changes to the floor above were even more ambitious. Tom and Bill had the roof raised to allow for 10-ft. ceilings in the rooms on that story. While the front elevation of the 1916 house appears unchanged from the street, every room, upstairs and down, was transformed as dramatically as Cinderella's pumpkin.

Tom and Bill had three goals—reconfigure the existing plan, restore the house to its original detailing, and selectively modernize the bathrooms, kitchen, and closets. They were not the only owners to have remodeled the house. The first major changes probably took place

It is not often you see wainscoting used in Bungalow living rooms, this feature being more commonly used in dining rooms or dens. But it works in this house, giving the living room the sumptuous feel of a private club.

FIRST FLOOR (AFTER)

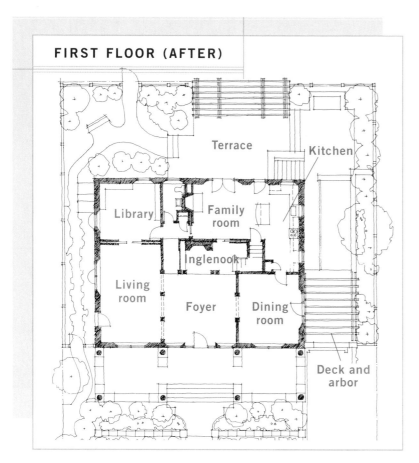

SECOND FLOOR (AFTER)

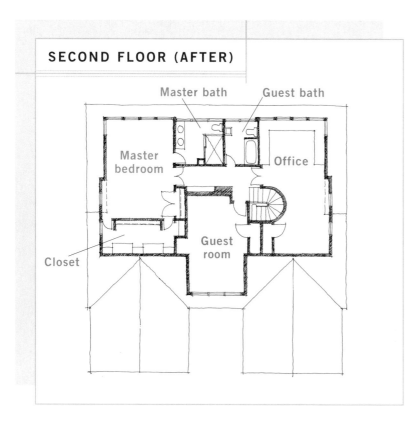

in the 1930s, during the streamlined Art Deco period, and much of the varnished woodwork was either replaced or painted white. In the 1970s, when the open plan was in vogue, the kitchen, butler's pantry, and dining room were all combined into one large room. Together, these projects had stripped the house down to its bare bones. So, how do you put a few "pounds" back on a house? By doubling up columns, restoring dark wood paneling, and employing various textures—wood, stone, and tile—throughout the house.

A Spaced-Out Plan

A critical aspect of this renovation was the designer's sophisticated layering of the spaces—that is, unfolding one space into another to create a delightful sequence of visual experiences as you walk through the house. Conventional design, in contrast, is concerned with the specifications of individual rooms and tends to overlook the way in which each room relates to the others. In this house, while no square footage was added to the first floor, the area feels greater because the eye (and the body) move freely through the plan. This openness has a practical function, too. The house can now handle either an intimate dinner party for six or a holiday reception for 106.

The foyer immediately impresses visitors with its formal appointments. Overhead, the heavy beams of the coffered ceiling are original to the house and, fortunately, were never painted or covered by a dropped acoustic-tile ceiling. The library is almost too inviting, with Craftsman lighting fixtures and bookshelves within

Literature, good lighting, and leisure time are the basic components of a home library. This library adds comfortable seating, well-designed bookshelves, and beautiful wood floors—elements that transform it from basic to classic.

This stone fireplace stoked the imagination of the owners. They knew this house was worth the time, expense, and effort it would take to renovate it.

pocket doors — Sliding doors that open by disappearing into spaces within specially built walls. Unlike conventional hinged doors, they don't obscure walls to either side of the doorway when open.

reach of the leather reading chairs. **Pocket doors** were common to original Bungalows, frequently used to close off the living room from the foyer and dining room, and all too often they were removed with the first round of remodeling changes. Today's owners are fortunate if they happen upon the old doors stashed away in the basement. The French pocket doors in Tom and Bill's house look like originals, but they are one of the many grace notes added with this project.

Tom and Bill's new kitchen incorporates the space formerly occupied by a pantry and now includes a cozy dining area with a view through the French doors to the loggia. The sophisticated urban garden has smooth flagstone pavers in the same color range as the rough-hewn stone of the house. Wood decking and arbors will weather to the gray tones of the wood shingles.

Navigating the original second floor was like following detour signs during road construction—you eventually got to where you were going, but it wasn't an easy trip. Doors banged into each other, the corridor between the bedrooms twisted and turned for no apparent reason, and while there is nothing unusual about a Bungalow second story with a low ceiling, this one had severe angles that made it difficult to walk into a room without bumping your head. And there just wasn't any place for the beds and dressers, because the rooms had so little unbroken wall space. With the sloped ceiling, closets, doors, and windows, where could they go?

ABOVE, **Halls tend to be** overlooked areas, but this one is both attractive and functional. The built-in storage and seating are conveniently located. Good ventilation helps relieve the sticky, still summer air of Washington, D.C., and the hall includes high operable windows, transoms over the doors, and ceiling fans.

LEFT, **The dark wood trim** of the original kitchen has been retained, making an attractive contrast to the bright work surfaces introduced by the remodeling.

ABOVE, **Lighting design** is a particularly important consideration for home offices. Recessed can fixtures and adjustable spots are used here to supplement a period desk lamp. By day, the added row of divided panes above the center windows brings in plenty of light.

RIGHT, **The heavy beams** and double columns are original to the house. This integral structural system made it easier to remove other, nonstructural walls.

Grafting Old to New

☆ **YOU'VE PROBABLY SEEN** additions that, as well loved as they may be, look something like front-end collisions. Before launching into an ambitious project, it is important to consider how the old and new portions of your Bungalow will get along with each other.

If you want to emphasize the changes, use contrasting materials, scales, or colors, while making sure that there is some continuity with the home's proportions and important horizontal lines. If you want to play it safe and have your changes blend in, repeat the existing theme. But what if you can't find new materials that suggest the home's mature look? In that case, try to match the new materials with those from another part of the house, some distance away from the construction.

To help old and new sit better with each other, you can employ a reveal, a surface set back or apart from an adjoining element in order to minimize the disruption of a seam. Just make sure that old and new surfaces are on different planes to minimize any unintentional difference in appearance.

Raising the Roof

In addressing these shortcomings, the second floor had to grow up in more ways than one, not only gaining height but also becoming more "grown up." Once Tom and Bill decided on the drastic (and expensive) move to raise the roof, they were free to reconfigure the rooms by moving walls, adding 280 sq. ft. in the process. They took a design cue from the front of the house and featured twin gable dormers in the back, linked by a wall of windows. One wing of the second floor was transformed into an expansive master suite with spacious walk-in closets, a master bath, and artful windows that turn the corner in a delightful way. With a nod to Bungalow tradition, the all-white tiled bathroom is the epitome of cleanliness, made all the brighter by the natural light washing in from a bank of windows.

The other wing became the home office, with two workstations. Nestled under the dormer, the work areas have ample daylight and ventilation, as well as a treetop view of the neighborhood. Two people can work comfortably, each with his own desk and computer space, file storage, and bookshelves. And yet the workstations are close enough to allow sharing a printer and brainstorming.

Tom and Bill's Bungalow shows just how far the style can be stretched to accommodate a modern plan. In the right hands, the result lets the personality of the homeowners come through, rather than an accumulation of design details.

Living Better Eclectically

P AT AND DAN BOUGHT A MODEST TWO-BEDROOM 1925 Bungalow along with the adjoining empty lot and its pair of 150-year-old burr oaks. The house was small—it may have been a mail-order product— and the beautiful neighboring property was the major impetus for making the purchase. Although Pat and Dan live in Minnesota, known as "the Land of 10,000 Lakes," the house isn't on water, and they conceived of the backyard as a big grassy "lake" to be viewed through large, new expanses of glass.

The house had its limitations—plain, simple, and functionally obsolete are the terms Dan used to describe it. Most of the windows faced north—not a good choice in Minneapolis, a cold city where passive solar heating is feasible because the area enjoys more hours of winter sunlight than most cities at that latitude. The kitchen was a cramped galleylike space, and the steep stair to the second floor was crammed into the hallway leading to the bathroom.

Pat and Dan took their time during the planning phase because their goals were ambitious. They wanted to double the square footage, including office space for

ABOVE, **This large, open kitchen** was made possible by removing the original staircase. Sometimes, you have to make radical decisions to get the quality of space you want.

LEFT, **The site can dictate** the scale of a new addition. The large oak trees help disguise the fact that the owners doubled the square footage of the original Bungalow.

Pat's real estate business, while making the most of the sunlight and the lot's views. And they wanted the new addition to continue the Bungalow style.

A Home Office Complex

Although the original house is recognizable from the outside, the rooms within have been completely redone. Pat's own office occupies the former living room, a little space from which was taken to enlarge the first-floor bathroom. Both the former sunroom and one of the back bedrooms serve as additional offices.

The new kitchen, with its two-toned wood cabinets, restoration hardware, and stainless-steel appliances, is a far cry from the original tiny, dark, and outdated facility. Dan and Pat expanded the kitchen by incorporating a

former bedroom, made possible by removing the skinny, steep stair that had divided them. The floors in the kitchen are maple, a lighter wood than used for the floors in the more formal rooms, and it contrasts well with the cabinets. The kitchen includes a casual dining area, graced by oversize double-hung windows that extend almost to the floor and provide a terrific view to the grassy "lake" area.

Bungalows have relaxed floor plans that don't waste space on unneeded hallways. But because this house was intended to serve both as office and home, a generous hallway was included to create a measure of separation between work area and living quarters. The hall creates a feeling of compression that sets off the spaciousness of the rooms beyond. The waiting area is filled

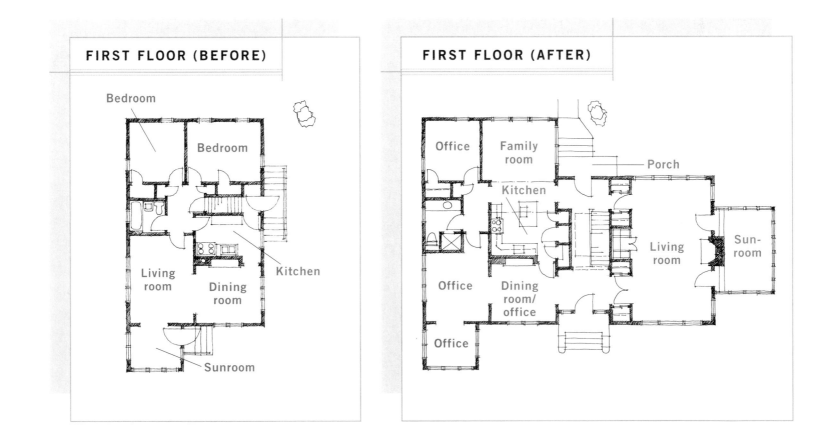

FIRST FLOOR (BEFORE)

Bedroom
Bedroom
Living room
Dining room
Kitchen
Sunroom

FIRST FLOOR (AFTER)

Office
Family room
Porch
Kitchen
Office
Dining room/ office
Living room
Sun-room
Office

Spare That Tree!

TREES ARE MORE THAN an attractive backdrop for a house. They cool and clean the air in summer, cast welcome shade over the lawn and patio, and protect the house from winter winds. Trees give value to your property that even an appraiser or home insurance agent could appreciate.

When planning an addition on a site with trees, consult with a landscape architect or an arborist to identify any trees that may be weak, diseased, or past their prime, with an eye to removing them. Before construction begins, make sure that your contractor and any subcontractors understand which trees are to be kept.

On a wooded lot, removing the sick, scrub, and volunteer trees will allow you to reveal specimen trees—attractive, well-formed examples of durable species that have been smothered by overgrowth. This is a relatively quick and inexpensive way to achieve an instant mature landscape.

with small details and nooks and crannies intended to hold a visitor's interest.

Keeping in Character

While it can be tempting to cover a stucco home with vinyl siding, for reasons of cost, insulation value, and ease of maintenance, Pat and Dan chose against compromising the home's character. Matching the addition to the existing stucco proved to be expensive, but it succeeded in creating a seamless look. This was one of the cost overruns that can be expected in almost every construction project for any number of reasons: a change in scope, unavailability of an inexpensive option, or an upgrade of materials. Even with several design revisions in the name of economy, this remodeling went 30 percent over budget.

Rather than compromise on the quality of the building materials (and with the goal of meeting the deadline), Pat and Dan decided that building a master suite would have to wait until Phase Two. In the meantime, they can take satisfaction in the quality of the job. The materials are nearly as exacting as in a true preservation—a red oak dining room floor, custom windows throughout, oak wall paneling, oak trim to replace painted features, custom molding with **dentils,** handcrafted tiles surrounding the fireplace, and antique lighting fixtures.

Pat and Dan's object wasn't to preserve a significant historical property but to be guided loosely by history. The many details, as Dan puts it, are "a nod to tradition but an eclectic mix and not specific to any time or place."

dentils Small square design elements used in a molding.

This entry does double duty, welcoming both friends and clients to the home office. With business in mind, this foyer is more formal and elaborate than is typical of most Bungalow entries.

Restoring Warmth

ABOVE, **This detached two-car garage** is in California, the home of car culture, and yet it manages to look more like an attractive garden structure than a garage.

FACING PAGE, **Colors interact** with each other in interesting ways. The purple and gray-blue of the paint palette picks up on the hues in the heavy stone retaining wall and the pattern of the paving. The crisp bright white of the trellis lifts your eyes to the diamond panes in the hallmark Bungalow dormer.

C HARLES AND NANNETTE'S 1906 BUNGALOW IS located in the quiet northern California town of Ross, a community that somehow has resisted the booming development taking place all around it. The old homes are remodeled and repaired—most of them Bungalows, with a scattering of Victorian and Cottage architecture. Nannette says that living in Ross gives her a sense of what life was like years ago. Giant trees shade the streets, and at dusk neighbors stroll down the old streets and chat over their fences.

Although the home had been altered many times over the years, it still had the small dormers that animate many Bungalow roofs, including diamond-shaped panes that add a fairy tale touch to the windows. The interior was a different story. Very little original detailing remained. Only the ghost of an outline on the walls hinted at where the elaborate wood trim had been. The simple trim that remained was covered up by white paint. Instead of finding beautiful wood under the carpeting, the new owners were disappointed to see floors so battered that they would have to be replaced.

These new casement windows are unusually large for a dormer, and they run around the sides as well. The three-over-one configuration, common to Bungalows, is used throughout the house.

box beams — Large exposed ceiling beams that may or may not be structural. They are used in Bungalows to make the ceiling seem lower and the home more intimate.

Building Within the Shell

By the time all the walls were stripped down to the studs in preparation for replacing the weakened foundation, Charles and Nannette realized they were not merely restoring an old house but building a largely new one within a shell. This had the positive effect of freeing them to blend modern with traditional. Rather than faithfully re-create an authentic Bungalow kitchen that hadn't existed for many years, they opted for an open-plan design that flows into the breakfast room. The granite-topped island and counters provide ample preparation space, doubling as elegant tabletops for appetizers and wine tasting when the party won't budge from the kitchen. **Box beams,** featured in many original Bungalow living rooms and used elsewhere in this house, have been called on to enliven what could have been a plain drywall ceiling. The kitchen makes use of

In California, the tradition of using local materials was stronger than with Bungalows back East, where fireplaces typically were made of standard brick. This new hearth uses the same type of stones found in the garden walls.

This California Bungalow really understands its heritage. The new wraparound veranda brings the *bangala* feel back to the Bungalow. You can enter the veranda from many rooms in the house; the indoor/outdoor flow is seamless.

quartersawn — The perpendicular angle to the log at which boards are sawn. Quartersawn oak is highly popular for Bungalow floors, trim, and period furniture because the wood's distinctive grain is emphasized.

lintel — A horizontal member that typically supports a load above an opening.

both recessed ceiling lighting and a traditional-looking brass fixture over the island, blending history and modern convenience.

A great help in the couple's restoration was finding a specialty line of period doors and windows. The consistent use of one type of window and door throughout the house provided them with a theme that helps tie the design together. They chose windows of Douglas fir, a wood native to the area that glows with a reddish blonde hue. The floors that had to be ripped out were replaced by **quartersawn** oak.

The large stones and massive **lintels** of the family room fireplace make something of a statement about building for the ages. In true California Bungalow tradition, the landscape is integrated into the living spaces and can be seen through the windows and doors flanking the fireplace.

A Hipped Bedroom

The master suite revels in the odd shapes dictated by the **hipped roof,** an unusual sight on a Bungalow. The ridge beam overhead is similar to the beams used downstairs. Another feature linking the two floors is the three-over-one pattern of the windows; here, casements are used, while the windows downstairs are both casements and double-hung.

Outside, this renovation incorporates an expansive veranda that goes far beyond the scope of a front porch; it wraps halfway around the Bungalow to add a layer of enclosure and living space between the house and garden. The Bungalow is painted a soft gray, coupled with trim of blue-spruce green and a pine-bark red front door as an accent.

The garage and a rental cottage stay close to the detailing and color choices of the house, so that the three structures work together as a little compound. Like the house, the garage has a distinctive hipped roof and even a tiny dormer of its own.

A renovation can have any of several types of goals—to add living area, to make rooms less formal, to modernize. In this house, Charles and Nannette have chosen to focus on something not quite as defined: restoring the warm feeling of a bygone era. This theme is abstract—more of a feeling than something you can see on a floor plan—and as a result the home has taken on the especially personal reflection of its owners.

hipped roof — A roof with four sloping, intersecting sides.

The bathroom vanity, like the home's kitchen island, has **the look of traditional cabinetry.** Placed under a skylight, the deep porcelain tub is the main event in this room.

The Bungalow Palette

bungalow style

AN EXTERIOR PAINT SCHEME can take your Bungalow beyond the ordinary—or beyond your neighbors' idea of what's proper. Instead of choosing hues in the paint store, consider the colors of the roof, nearby plantings, and houses along the street.

For inspiration (and to limit the near-infinite combinations of color choices), it helps to research original paint schemes in old pattern books and current books on the Bungalow style. Best of all, walk around Bungalow neighborhoods

and take notes and photographs. With some luck, you may find a home that already displays the very color combination you have in mind.

Here are a few tips on testing colors, taken from our own struggles to find just the right shade:

• Scan a color photo of your Bungalow into your computer, then add various schemes with a graphics program.
• Print photocopies of a line drawing of your home, then use color pencils to experiment.

• Spend the extra money to buy a pint of each sample color and test it, either on a small area of the house itself or on a piece of scrap plywood.

Before scraping or sanding the paint of an older house, have your building inspector check it for lead content. Lead can be a serious health hazard, especially if ingested by small children. Follow the recommendations of the inspector or your local health department.

Third Time
Is the Charm

ABOVE AND FACING PAGE, **The front** of this Bungalow was closely restored to resemble its original condition (above). The shingled dormer, with windows on three sides, was originally a sleeping porch.

C HARLOTTE'S ARLINGTON, VIRGINIA, BUNGALOW is a manufactured house, one of more than 100,000 sold by Sears, Roebuck and Co. between 1908 and 1940. (And today we think buying used guitars and lamps on eBay is futuristic!) There was nothing shoddy about the construction of these houses, and they have become well loved by generations of owners. Charlotte chose to rebuild her Bungalow to closely resemble the original design—twice, the second time after the newly remodeled house was damaged in a major fire.

Manufactured Bungalows were built of high-quality materials. The less-expensive models were put together as carefully as top-of-the-line houses, the main differences being size and interior finishes. Some Sears homes were very roomy, with four bedrooms and two-and-a-half baths, while others lacked indoor bathrooms. Many residential neighborhoods—in mining and company towns in particular—had a high percentage of manufactured homes.

Seeing the Potential

Even homes that were originally built to last require routine maintenance, and Charlotte's house was definitely in need of attention when she bought it. The

Renovations can blend in better with the original house if they include vintage touches, such as this newel post anchoring the home's new stair.

wood window frames and fascia boards were rotting, the tiled roof needed to be replaced, and the rear elevation was an amalgam of disjointed porches. The garage was too small even for one car, and it was listing so badly that it had become unusable. The site slopes to the back, with several level changes. As a result, the house was perched awkwardly, contrary to the way in which Bungalows usually snuggle into the landscape, and the basement wall was exposed in an ungainly way. Although there was plenty of potential for a lovely garden behind the house, only one window faced that way. Still, with all of these liabilities, the house retained much of its charm, the yard had possibilities, and the neighborhood was terrific. Charlotte decided to invest in a major remodeling.

FIRST FLOOR (BEFORE)

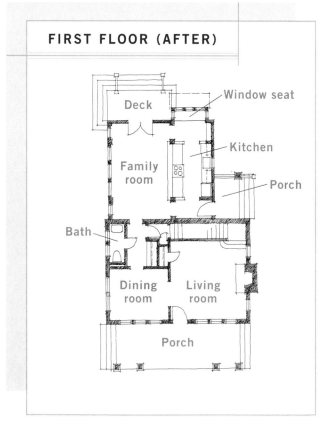

FIRST FLOOR (AFTER)

ABOVE, **A family room** is not always the appropriate solution for family togetherness. This small "away" space allows the cook to bustle about in the kitchen while the company is comfortably out of the way.

LEFT, **The tidy geometric grid** of these shelves is just the right size to showcase a collection but not so large that it becomes a catchall. This new built-in fits in well with nearby traditional appointments, including the window seat and divided-light windows.

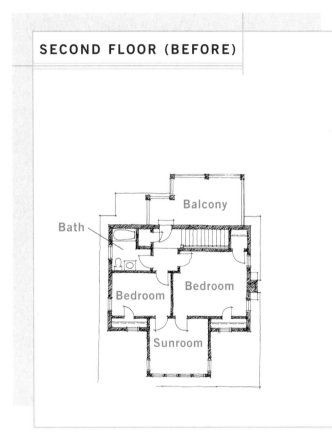

SECOND FLOOR (BEFORE)

Bath

Balcony

Bedroom

Bedroom

Sunroom

SECOND FLOOR (AFTER)

Balcony

Master bedroom

Bath

Bedroom

Bedroom

Sunroom

An Arlington Phoenix

Charlotte hired the firm of Morris-Day Designers and Builders to design the project. Work was completed just before the winter holidays and then the fire broke out. Charlotte set about rebuilding immediately. Six intense months later, she invited Dwight and her friends to celebrate this second renovation with a big house party.

Were the results worth living through two renovations? Absolutely. Charlotte increased the square footage of her home by 60 percent, going from two bedrooms and one bath to three bedrooms and two-and-a-half baths. The addition takes full advantage of the newly landscaped backyard, with a second-floor balcony overlooking the flagstone patio and flower garden. The yard

is easily reached from the interior through French doors. The new two-car garage looks more fitting for a Bungalow than the original did. It borrows both the articulated double knee braces and shingles from the house. The finely scaled divided lights over the garage doors are a particularly nice touch, again matching the character of the house.

A testimony to the charm of the original Bungalow is that the remodeling was based so closely on it, right down to the enclosed sleeping porch on the second floor. Inside, despite the water and smoke damage, the house retains such Bungalow hallmarks as built-ins, box beams, and the traditional half-wall between front rooms. The ideas behind the Bungalow style proved to be invulnerable to both time and fire.

ABOVE AND LEFT, **Prior to the addition**, the backyard was inaccessible from the house (left). The new construction took advantage of the sloped site, with a deck and patio that gracefully take up the grade change.

You Don't
Have to Leave

The two windows flanking the fireplace look as though they are original to the house, but they are new, added to give the fireplace wall a more traditional Bungalow look.

double-gabled ⁀A side of the house that has two gables, adding visual interest.

F

EW NEIGHBORHOODS ARE STRICTLY ALL Bungalows, and this renovation combines its Bungalow bloodlines with a suggestion of the more vertical, two-story Four Square houses along the street. Joanne's house was originally a one-story, 950-sq.-ft. home with a **double-gabled** front—a major and a minor gable faced the street. It was small and quite ordinary. But the wraparound porch provided a gracious entry, the neighborhood was pleasant, and Joanne decided in favor of remodeling instead of moving.

Since the house is on a corner lot, setbacks dictated that the only place an addition could go was up. Joanne still wanted the addition to retain the character of the original house. The wide, major gable was rebuilt, while the new second story appears as the minor gable above.

A House Has Zones

Dwight McNeil, of Morris-Day Designers and Builders, was called in. At the outset, he stated the obvious—that the second floor would become the private zone, freeing the entire first floor to serve as a public area for

Bungalows were often built on tight lots, and setbacks may dictate that the only way to gain more space is to go up. The exterior lines of this original Bungalow can still be traced under the massing of the added second-floor forms.

Strictly speaking, this new house is no longer a Bungalow but more like a cousin related by marriage. There are many reasons for large additions, including keeping pace with rising property values in the neighborhood.

FIRST FLOOR (BEFORE)

Porch

Kitchen

Bedroom

Bath

Dining room

Living room

Bedroom

Porch

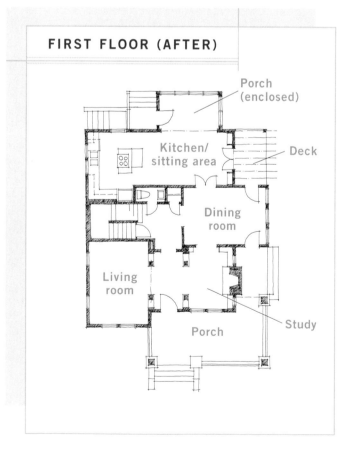

FIRST FLOOR (AFTER)

Porch (enclosed)

Kitchen/ sitting area

Deck

Dining room

Living room

Study

Porch

family gatherings and entertaining. As simple as this concept of zoning may seem, it often is hard for home-owners to visualize these changes in function because they are so familiar with the existing layout.

The square footage of the house more than doubled, giving Joanne the space for having large parties downstairs while bedrooms and baths gained privacy on the floor above. Yet the house retains the small-scale feel that attracted her to it in the first place. It may no longer be a pedigree Bungalow on the outside, but the rooms within are a contemporary translation of the Bungalow vocabulary.

Just as important as dramatically increasing the living space was altering the perception of spaciousness. Dwight took a sculptural approach to reconfiguring the downstairs. In a subtractive way, he carved out sections

SECOND FLOOR (AFTER)

Master bedroom

Bath

Bedroom

Bedroom

Bungalow dining rooms are special. They are the most formal rooms in the house, setting the tone for sit-down dinners where the family and guests linger for coffee and conversation.

The worktable in this kitchen resembles the old fat-legged butcher's tables. This contemporary kitchen weaves in other references to the Bungalow era, with wood wainscoting, wood floors, and a black-and-white color scheme.

of the walls to create a top, middle, and base to the
rooms, so that you are aware of the entire area of the
first floor when walking through it. The woodwork is
in character for a Bungalow, and yet it all has been
painted white to arrive at the uncluttered look that was
important to the owner. The tilework of the fireplace,
with its grid of alternating earthy colors, also has a
decidedly modern feel, contrasting nicely with the art-
glass windows.

An all-white Bungalow interior
is not traditional, but many new
owners choose to lighten the
household scheme for an open,
cheery look. A relatively flat
white paint also heightens the
architectural sense of things,
such as these tapered columns
and the beams they support.

Wedding a House to Its Site

Joanne's original house didn't take full advantage of its
terrific sunny location. Dwight's solution was to wrap
the porch around the corner to the dining room. This
horizontal layering helps to keep the second-floor addition from appearing too vertical. Also, a new door from
the dining room allows diners to drift out to the porch
and patio, tying the outdoor entertainment spaces to

The addition adds three new doorways into the garden from the house. The easier it is to flow in and out of the house, the quicker a yard becomes a garden.

☆ # Hearth and Home

BUNGALOW LIVING ROOMS were often accentuated with fireplaces surrounded by wood detailing and even inglenook seating, making it clear that this was the center of home life. Some were built with fake fireplaces, perhaps because homeowners wanted to avoid the mess of dragging in firewood and dealing with ashes. (Our Bungalow fireplace had fake pine logs on a brass andiron, illumi- nated by a flickering orange bulb—we would have pre- ferred the mess!)

Adding a functional fire- place to an existing Bunga- low can be a challenge. Most wood-burning fireplaces have a firebox and a vertical flue with a noncombustible surround. By code, the flue should extend at least 3 ft. above the roof. The exposed top of the flue may need to be covered; check with your local design review board. Gas-fired fireplaces are simpler to install and can involve running a flue horizontally out of the firebox to the exterior.

the adjacent rooms. A fringe benefit is that the house seems even larger than its actual square footage. The design challenge here was to make the connection between inside and outside as convenient as possible so that guests naturally drift outside without giving it a second thought.

Joanne's old kitchen was a galley affair, with no room for friends to keep the cook company. The new room provides places for the guests to sit while pitching in to help. The wood floors, with their natural finish, have a traditional look that warms up the kitchen's bold black, white, and chrome finishes (see the photo on p. 128). Three types of lighting—recessed ceiling lights, pendant lighting, and under-the-cabinet fixtures—all work in concert to make the room glow softly but brightly enough to illuminate the task at hand. Kitchen lighting can be tricky to get just right, and you may want to talk with your architect about calling in a lighting designer specifically for this room.

A mark of the success of this remodeling is that it looks as though it must have happened decades ago. Credit the yard for this, in part. The newly expanded house is framed by the mature trees overhead and newly planted extensive shrubs and flower beds on all sides. When this level of care goes into the plantings, a house can be the expression of its site.

The master bathroom on the new second floor retains a traditional vocabulary. The tilework and the profile of the window frame evoke the Bungalow style, while the wainscoting adds a Victorian note.

What Were They Thinking?

Borrowing heavily from the detailing on the original Bungalow, this new gable displays a carefully organized hierarchy of structural members that focuses attention on the home's entry.

A S YOU PASS BY A HOME WITH AN AWKWARD addition, you may find yourself wondering, "What were they thinking? What did the house look like when it was built?" We call this subtractive process "erasure architecture," and it can be helpful in focusing on the strong points of your house as you consider your own remodeling plans.

Jean and Randy bought this 1924 Maryland Bungalow because they liked the older neighborhood and thought the interior plan would work well for their family. The problem was the exterior. Each of the previous owners had set off on a remodeling project that, while providing great interior living spaces, compromised the architectural integrity of the Bungalow.

As Jean and Randy raised their family, they occasionally thought about ways in which they could "subtract" the home's unfortunate changes and bring back its Bungalow character. But it wasn't until they retired and their children were off on their own that they finally had time to go ahead with a renovation. One of their children, Julia, is an architect, and she understood both the Bungalow philosophy and her parents' personal style.

The architect turned to the Bungalow hallmark of the wraparound porch to knit together the disparate additions of this 1924 Maryland Bungalow. Restoring a Bungalow porch can be a unifying feature for a Bungalow that has been modernized beyond recognition.

Bungalow staircases in living rooms were more common on the East Coast than in the Midwest, where they were typically located off the kitchen, or on the West Coast, where one-story Bungalows prevailed.

A Unifying Strategy

The three worked closely to regain the 1920s character of the house without compromising the livable interior. For their part, Randy and Jean researched the history of their home, and along the way they discovered a similar Bungalow, The Walton, illustrated in *Houses by Mail: A Guide to Houses from Sears, Roebuck and Company*, by Katherine Cole Stevenson and H. Ward Jandl. The book was a great help in establishing what the house looked like before its many alterations. But because the house had been so transfigured over the years, Julia convinced her parents that unraveling all of the changes would be impractical. Rather than start from scratch, the best approach would be to knit all the pieces together with one big, bold idea.

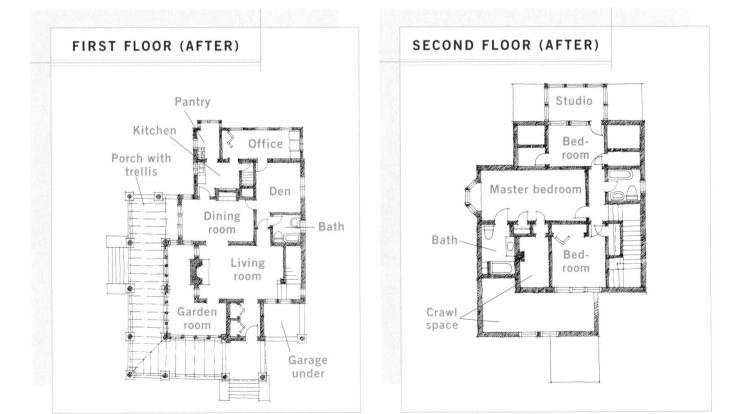

FIRST FLOOR (AFTER)

Pantry
Kitchen
Office
Porch with trellis
Den
Dining room
Bath
Living room
Garden room
Garage under

SECOND FLOOR (AFTER)

Studio
Bedroom
Master bedroom
Bath
Bedroom
Crawl space

The new porch addition, with its brick, stone, tile, and overarching beams, adds hundreds of square feet of outdoor living space to this home. Wisteria vines wind around the columns for early summer scent, seasonal shade, and a romantic structure to capture snowflakes.

Jean and Randy had a suggestion. During their research, they had found themselves returning again and again to the works of Frank Lloyd Wright and Greene and Greene, houses that beautifully interact with the outdoors. They decided that this connection was the critical design element missing from their home. In response, Julia designed a wraparound porch, complete with trellis and terraces.

Paying careful attention to the materials of the original house, Julia took great pains to find the right match for the brick, paint, and columns. As a result, the new porch looks as though it has always been a part of the house. In fact, the house seems to spring from it, so well integrated are the changes Julia designed. The twining wisteria is an example of a plant that is appropriate to both the Bungalow style and to Maryland's climate. This choice set the tone for the rest of the landscape design.

CHAPTER FOUR

BRAND-NEW BUNGALOWS

ABOVE, **Owners of brand-new** Bungalows still expect—and get—high-quality craftsmanship.

FACING PAGE, **This Iowa** Bungalow follows Frank Lloyd Wright's dictum that homes in the prairie should rise out of a hill, not sit on top of it.

NEW BUNGALOW? EVEN TO THE MOST DEVOTED Bungalow owner, the two words together sound strange. Bungalows belong in old neighborhoods, on tree-lined streets. They are small, quaint, and have a charming patina of darkened varnish, weathered brick, and wood. They are "fixer-uppers," aren't they?

Yes…and no. Once again, new Bungalows are cropping up coast to coast. While this second wave of Bungalow building can't quite be termed "Bungalow Mania," it is clear that the style continues to suit our contemporary life. These new houses take full advantage of modern building materials and construction techniques, and yet the hallmarks—a low-lying house with a big roof sweeping down to include a front porch—come through loud and clear.

Why Build New?

Assuming you've been paging through this book from front to back, you've seen lots of appealing older homes. Given that there are so many handsome, updated Bungalows in pleasant neighborhoods, you might wonder why anyone would want to go through the demanding process of building a new one.

There are several good reasons to build a new Bungalow. Just as many single people lament that all the "good ones" are taken, special Bungalows in great neighborhoods don't come on the real estate market frequently. You may have tired of waiting for that perfect Bungalow and decided to take your future into your own hands. Or you may be one of those people who simply prefers to have new things—cars, tools, furniture—without the associations of other past owners and other times. While some people prefer the idea of

owning a lived-in house with a built-in history, others want a place that looks, smells, and feels freshly minted. But the best reason of all, we think, is that the Bungalow with its compact floor plan is a perfect expression of the popular concept of The Not So Big House, espoused by author and architect Sarah Susanka.

A new home also gives you plenty of opportunity for self-expression. Rather than inherit the problems and fixes of past owners, you can design and build a home from the ground up. Building your own home is an ambitious project that will benefit from all the attention and energy you can invest in it. The result is guaranteed to express who you are in a highly visible way.

When the topic of new construction comes up, most people think of suburban or rural locations. Not all new homes are built in outlying areas. After years of

New construction
includes housing for the car, if not two or three. In this house, the large dimensions of the garage provide the perfect footprint for a second-story guest suite.

migration to the suburbs, both empty nesters and young families are returning to the city and rediscovering the joys of urban living. Infill housing—a term that means building new houses on vacant city lots in existing neighborhoods—is enjoying great popularity. City lots can be less expensive than exurban lots, the infrastructure is already in place, and the lots are smaller and don't require hours of maintenance. Many families enjoy the proximity to urban cultural, recreational, and mass-transit opportunities. The typical urban lot, with its 19th-century dimensions (as small as 45 ft. by 100 ft.), lends itself to Bungalow construction. The traditional Bungalow detailing fits right into an older neighborhood with its mix of Colonial, Cape, and Victorian housing styles.

Two new Bungalows blend in with two older Bungalows in this California neighborhood. The popular housing style is sailing into a new century.

Universal Design

WHEN BUILDING a new home or addition, think ahead about making it accessible to disabled people— even if you yourself are relatively young and ambulatory. Consider that almost everyone is disabled at some point over a life span. Ever since Louis broke both an arm and a leg in a skating accident a few years ago, we have been keenly aware of the need to draw up plans with accessibility in mind.

In new construction, bathroom walls can be blocked, adding extra frame members or plywood to anchor grab bars now or in the future. Hallways and doorways should be made wide enough to accommodate a wheelchair. Conventional doorknobs can be replaced with lever sets for ease of operation. Some alterations are more involved. An accessible kitchen can be a large and costly undertaking, with such features as a drop sink and lowered counters and base cabinets.

In the larger scheme of things, you may want to make it possible for a person to live solely on the first floor in order to avoid steps. Most Bungalows provide a den or studio space that can double as a temporary bedroom. To provide access to the house, a ramp can be sensitively integrated with the entry. Exterior lifts are expensive, may be difficult to merge with the home's design, and are somewhat vulnerable to the weather. Finally, check if your community provides tax incentives or credits to assist in making homes accessible.

By focusing views to the distant landscape, the owners of this Washington State Bungalow can almost forget that they have neighbors close on either side.

Building a new home with a traditional facade allows you to follow the Bungalow philosophy of fitting in architecturally while including labor-saving devices and up-to-the-minute technology. It is a daunting task to make an older home energy efficient. Building new affords you the opportunity of building a home that is well insulated and includes the latest in efficient heating and cooling systems.

If you choose to build in the countryside, will your Bungalow look out of place? Not at all. In fact, the wide range of Bungalow styles, from Spanish to Japanese, indicates that Bungalows are one of the most adaptable of building styles. A hallmark of Bungalow style is a strong connection to the outdoors, and while Bungalows are good city neighbors, they are also terrific country cousins.

Choose Your Strategy

There are many ways to go about designing and building a new home, all of which have pros and cons. The most important requirement may be to find a design professional with whom you can clearly communicate and place your trust. Building a new home requires a leap of faith. You are about to launch into one of the most expensive projects of a lifetime. And you really don't know exactly what you are going to end up with until you give the finished place a final sweep, with the smell of drying paint heavy in the air. That's true no matter how many drawings, models, or virtual tours you look at. Scary? Maybe. Exciting? Definitely!

This book includes examples of homes that are the result of working with various teams, including architects, developers, and contractors. A few families decide to go it alone, handling most of the phases of design and construction themselves. You may choose to have a

With its plentiful windows and plentiful porches, the Bungalow is at home in gentle climates. This new southern California house also uses French doors to tie an outdoor dining area with adjacent rooms.

Windows Worth Looking At

WINDOWS ARE key players in setting the Bungalow stage; they are relatively large and plentiful in this style and often grouped in units of two or three. All of that glass contributes to the spacious feel of a Bungalow's open plan. The wood trim surrounding the windows is a major feature of the room's character, and beveled or stained glass distinguishes many of these homes.

Most Bungalows were built with double-hung windows that were standard on other styles as well but often with a difference: The upper sash frequently was divided into three or four vertical panes (or lights). Traditional double-hungs have their drawbacks. It is difficult to clean the glass, to replace broken sash cords and panes, and to free a sticking sash. New models tilt, rotate, or slide to make cleaning and maintenance easier. The glass itself can be made with high-tech coatings and multipane thermal glazing to improve energy efficiency and reduce glare.

Some window types are less sympathetic to the Bungalow—very large picture and arch-topped windows, in particular. Instead, you may want to specify double-hung, casement, or awning windows, possibly with a pattern of individual panes that match what was used on the original house.

Selecting colors for new windows can be tricky because each window manufacturer has its own variations. With something as visible as a window, you don't want to be saddled with "last year's color." Custom colors are an extra-cost option. Personally, we think that strong and distinctive colors add visual punch to a traditional facade, but it is always a safe bet to choose a neutral color if you are buying vinyl- or metal-clad windows with a factory-applied color finish.

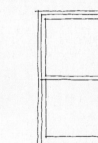

Double-hung

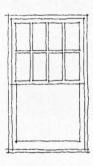

Eight-over-one
double-hung

Nine-over-one
double-hung

Prairie style

Arch top

Bungalow designed specifically for you, but custom projects make up a very small percentage of new homes. Most are standardized designs, from commercially available plans. Some architectural firms don't even design houses for individual clients but specialize in speculative work, designing a house for typical, composite clients—for example, a couple with two kids, three cars, and a certain income level.

Coming Up with a Plan

Nearly every kid has done a drawing (perhaps on the margins of homework) of the perfect house. Chances are it resembles a castle, with secret passageways and a moat filled with crocodiles. Later, as adults, we start to identify the best (and worst) things about the places we've lived in to arrive at a more refined idea of a dream house.

If you choose to work with a design professional, bring your sketches to the preliminary planning sessions. Clients typically arrive at our office with a folder or scrapbook of photos torn from magazines, and more often than not these images represent dreams of a lifestyle, not the house itself. The pictures are seductive. We encourage would-be Bungalow owners to put the pictures away for awhile and instead think about the ways in which the configuration of the structure might support that lifestyle. Then, after the size and function of the house's areas are determined, the photos can come back out for inspiration on how to make the structure come to life.

Just as original Bungalow owners bought plans from manufacturers such as Sears or Montgomery Ward, you too can order both historic plans and updated versions (see Sources on p. 198). Many of the contemporary examples include drawings of garages, furniture, fur-

This large mantel boldly expresses the hearth, which is still the focus of Bungalow living rooms in brand-new Bungalows.

An illuminated newel post is an attractive and sculptural way to light the stairs.

nishings, and hardware appropriate to the style. Analyzing these plans is a good place to start your design process. Compare the sizes of the rooms to the rooms you currently are living in for a benchmark as to how those dimensions would look and feel. In this way, when you start laying out a plan, you'll have a frame of reference.

Studying published plans also can be a good exercise in learning how to read architectural drawings. This is an especially important skill whether you build your own home or act as the general contractor. And even if you decide to hire an architect, general contractor, or a design–build firm, a familiarity with drawings will help you understand the design process so that you can make better–informed decisions.

The Healthy House

MANY PEOPLE ARE LOOKING for a house that will promote wellness, and the Bungalow was an early attempt at providing a healthful environment for the family. These homes did a good job of bringing the outdoors in and opening rooms to the outdoors. Front porches, pergolas, and sun parlors were in-between living spaces, offering shelter from the elements and also fresh air and natural light. The sleeping porch was an unusual feature, open to cooling breezes and reputed to be an aid in resisting lung diseases.

Because window treatments were kept simple, they were less likely to trap dust than heavy, multi-layered drapes. Floors were ornamented with small decorative rugs, which could be taken out to the yard for a good beating. The tiled Bungalow bathroom was the epitome of hygiene. And the home's many built-ins made cleaning easier because there weren't as many freestanding pieces of furniture to sweep around and under.

Finally, the modest size of the Bungalow made it easier to maintain without a maid. There just weren't as many dark corners to trap dust and dirt—a big plus in ensuring the house doesn't aggravate allergies. None of these features was radical in itself, but together they describe a home for healthful living.

SET YOUR SIGHTS ON A LOT

Choosing a lot is a crucial part of building a home. It represents a large portion of your total construction budget, and the site will affect every other decision you make. You can improve a poor site with plantings and site engineering, but these solutions tend to be expensive.

The new Bungalows in this chapter once again show the style's adaptability. They are built on sloped sites, steep sites, wooded sites, and urban sites, from Washington State to Rhode Island. Even so, not all sites are equal, and here are some guidelines for choosing the best situation for your Bungalow.

The couple who live in this house were involved in every stage of design and construction, including looking for just the right handmade tiles for their kitchen.

Bungalow Bloodlines

PEOPLE OFTEN ASK US about the defining qualities of a Bungalow. Are there design rules? Which ones can you break or at least bend without losing that special something that Bungalows have?

There are a few basic features that identify a Bungalow. Most important is a well-designed plan that maximizes the flow of shared spaces, minimizes circulation, and capitalizes on the natural benefits of lighting and ventilation. There is its one-story appearance from the street; as shown by houses in the previous chapters, this doesn't mean the house can't expand to two full stories. A dormer usually moderates that highly visible roof. And in many houses, the roof extends to encompass a generous front porch.

As for the building materials, they may be low-tech—brick, wood, shingle, stone—but they should also be regionally produced. The front door is apt to be something special, perhaps a one-of-a-kind design that helps to set this Bungalow apart from all others. And there probably will be plenty of windows, often grouped together rather than spaced evenly apart as they would be in a Cape or Colonial.

Of course, these are just the pieces. The charm of a Bungalow is in the way the pieces are all brought together.

A sloped site can be more visually pleasing than a relatively flat one, but it may require the expense of stairs and retaining walls as well as the services of a landscape architect or civil engineer. Then there are the practical concerns of accessibility. Will your home be accessible after a skiing accident or for an aging parent who moves in? Could a ramp be discreetly added to your home without jeopardizing the integrity of the Bungalow style? A slope toward the house may direct water into the basement—and one thing you want to avoid at all costs is a wet basement. Will basement windows be above grade, or will they need lightwells? Where will the driveway and garage door be in relation to the slope?

Is the site completely covered with great towering trees? Big trees are attractive, act as a windbreak, and can cool the house in summer, but you may want some rooms to be flooded with natural light for at least part of the day. And what about enjoying sunlight on a patio or setting aside some lawn for an outdoor play space? Even if you want your site to remain heavily wooded, it will be necessary to cut down some trees to make way for heavy construction equipment.

A crucial element (and one that you may have little control over) is future development. Give special consideration to plans for building on the land between you and your view. People often forget that a housing lot is part of a larger landscape, with its patterns of drainage, sunlight, wind, and traffic noise—and potential construction. Go to the offices of your local municipality and look at the area's **comprehensive plan.** Is the lovely wildflower meadow across the street slated for a condominium project or a shopping center? Does the developer have the right to build on a community's shared open space after a certain number of years?

What are the height limitations for future buildings? Are there any plans for widening the road or adding a new highway?

Making a sound decision on siting the house may involve a team—landscape architect, arborist, architect, and builder. Working together, they can reduce the impact of construction on the property, save the desirable plantings, make the most of cooling breezes, screen the poor views, and celebrate any vistas you may be fortunate enough to have. Remember, the views from the interior of the house are just as important as the views to the house.

By building a new house in an established neighborhood, you know where the good views are and can plan windows accordingly. In this home, larger windows were placed to take advantage of attractive vistas.

comprehensive plan—A local or regional area's determination of how it will change and grow over a designated period.

A Woodsy Bungalow

While the great majority of Bungalows are on lots with little or no grade, this house takes full advantage of the sloping site. The entry stair is very close to the street, but its porch and patio hover high in the air, creating sheltered, private spaces with great views.

Although Bungalows lend themselves to almost any sort of lot, there are certain settings that just seem to cry out for a Bungalow. That was the experience of Michelle and Brian, who bought a small wooded property in Laguna Beach, a village on the California coast with an artsy reputation. The area's new houses tend to be large and contemporary, but the couple thought that the older Bungalows in their neighborhood were perfect for the area, and they were inspired to build one of their own.

Before Michelle and Brian thought about the room configuration and roof pitches of the new design, they sat down and discussed just what it was they wanted from a house. They agreed it was important to make the most of the views. They decided to surround themselves with simple but beautiful materials. And they were determined to make the most of their sloped lot.

Deceptively Small

The resulting house is bigger than it appears, principally because it rises out of the sloping grade. The fieldstone retaining walls make the house look as though it is

Part of the appeal of the Bungalow style is a lack of pretension, but as shown in this house, that doesn't mean doing without rich materials and elegant details. The beam, the mantel, and the hearth are all custom built to the proportions of the house, ensuring that the scale is just right.

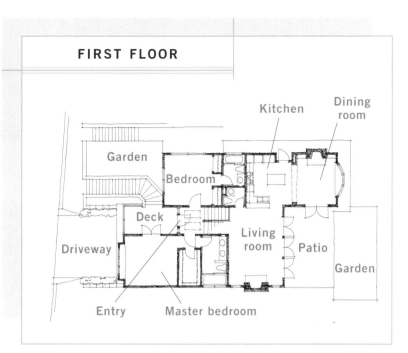

growing naturally out of the hillside. The pitch is just right to allow slipping in a two-car garage underneath the house—one way to ensure that the garage is conveniently located but does not overwhelm the small-scale house. The couple took advantage of the attractive garage doors that recently have appeared on the market, doors that are designed to complement the architecture of older (or older-looking) houses.

The impressive stone steps, with their substantial cedar handrails, were designed to make an event out of arriving at the house. A generous landing encourages visitors to pause, catch their breath, and admire the view before approaching the front. On clear days, the ocean is visible beyond the foothills.

In line with Brian and Michelle's design goals, the entry was constructed with superior materials, simply expressed. The paneled wood door has stained-glass windows and a substantial iron door handle. The natural cedar shakes will weather to various soft shades of gray, but for now they gleam like copper. The roof overhang, with its attractively exposed rafter tails, provides a sense of enclosure even before you step inside. Only when you are well inside are the living and dining rooms

FACING PAGE AND RIGHT, **Building a narrow house on a steep slope allowed the owners to take full advantage of dramatic views, and the house seems the larger for it.**

The owners were able to display their own craftsmanship with a newel post that sets the tone for this small but artful Bungalow.

revealed—this Bungalow tells its eloquent story one page at a time.

Although the house is only 1,500 sq. ft., it seems larger—in part, because it embraces an additional 350 sq. ft. of porch and patio, carefully integrated into the floor plan. Michelle and Brian's house takes the California idea of indoor/outdoor living to a remarkable level. The majority of the home's windows are, in fact, French doors. This approach can save money, since windows tend to be more expensive than doors and

Warm Doors

AS THE SAYING GOES, "you never get a second chance to make a first impression," and that's worth keeping in mind when you consider replacing or refinishing the front door of your Bungalow. An original front door can be a mixed blessing if it needs to be replaced because it likely has nonstandard dimensions. Professional restoration or repair should be considered. But this is one time you shouldn't compromise on design, quality, or expense.

And you may not have to. If you live in a city with lots of Bungalows, you may be able to find an old door in an architectural salvage store. These doors can sometimes be cut down to fit a smaller opening, although not so drastically that they are weakened. You also might order a new Bungalow-style door through advertisements in home-building magazines or firms offering restoration products on the Internet. A new door has practical benefits: It will be more energy efficient and offer greater security, and it can be fitted easily with up-to-date hardware.

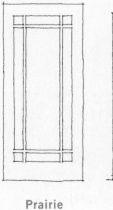 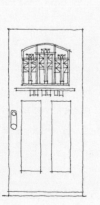 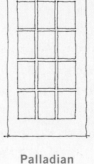  

Prairie   Craftsman   Palladian   Craftsman with sidelites   Twin panel 3/4 lite with single-panel sidelites

in southern California there are few concerns about insects and energy loss. The walls seem to dissolve when all the doors are open. The bedroom's double French doors open out to a stair, allowing views of the rising moon in the night sky. The living room and dining room can be made into something like a porch by opening the four sets of French doors to the patio.

Views are a dynamic element in the design of this Bungalow, another device that makes the compact home seem larger. Brian and Michelle took into account that other homes were being built around them, and they positioned windows to capture vistas that wouldn't be blocked by new construction.

A patio seamlessly links the living room and dining room. The patio furniture is all the more inviting because it is stylistically similar to the dining room table and chairs just inside.

In contrast to the transparency of the exterior walls, the couple has chosen the solid look of Mission-style furniture and interior detailing, along with a touch of Arts and Crafts. It was important for them, however, not to overwhelm the scale of the house with too much of a good thing. They were careful to keep a lot of white in the palette; this serves both to bounce light and also to show off the traditional Bungalow furnishings, mantel, handcrafted tiles, ceiling beam, hardwood floors, inlaid wood newel post, and paneled doors.

By slightly bumping out the window, this room was made to appear significantly larger. At night, the recessed low-voltage lighting in the soffit gives the window area a warm glow, alleviating the need for space-compressing window treatments.

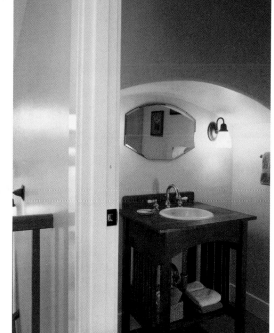

ABOVE, **In this tiny powder room,** slipped in just off the stair landing, a curved ceiling makes it obligatory for guests to bow in reverence to the Mission-style sink surround.

LEFT, **Some people** have to leave their homes to sleep in romantic rooms with great views; these homeowners built theirs in.

Deceptively New

An intimate scale does not mean doing without. Both the dining room and the living room are graced with their own fireplaces, each with distinctive tilework. The open kitchen is well equipped and efficient, with hanging pot and pan storage making decoration out of necessity. The kitchen flows into both living and dining rooms, making maximum use of the square footage and including the cooks in the surrounding activities.

Brian and Michelle were involved in a lot of the actual construction themselves, and they continue to add features that take time and skill. Brian is planning to build Arts and Crafts bookshelves on either side of the living room fireplace. Motivated by the advent of a new baby, they want to build a *casita* (Spanish for "a small house") in the backyard to double as either an adult retreat or a kid's playroom.

Brian says that at first he was offended when passersby would look at his brand-new Bungalow and ask, "What condition was this place in before you remodeled?" In time, he came to see this as a compliment. It affirmed that he and Michelle had achieved their goal of designing a new house with a sense of place, one that will age gracefully in the century ahead.

Northwest Prairie

ABOVE, **From the back,** this house looks entirely contemporary, but the dormer in the front elevation is a traditional Bungalow device, designed to make better use of the second floor while maintaining a low, modest profile.

FACING PAGE, **The graceful windows,** with their ornamental sidelights, frame the landscape in a picturesque way.

K EN DAHLIN OF GENESIS ARCHITECTURE IN Racine, Wisconsin, has a growing reputation for his up-to-the-minute interpretations of the Bungalow. He makes plans available to the public through home magazines, an encouraging sign that good architects are interested in making speculative houses accessible to the general public.

Ken's influences include those that helped shape the original Bungalows—the Prairie houses of Frank Lloyd Wright in the Midwest and Greene and Greene on the West Coast. In turn, the work of these firms reflected an interest in the Arts and Crafts Movement from England and in Japanese architecture, as expressed through the use of wood, stucco, and stone and traditional exposed joinery. There was an emphasis on hand-crafted ornament as well—glazed tile, cast terra-cotta, and art glass—and these became standard, even in unassuming homes.

Suited to Its Site

The architect's influences are on display in Sharon's Washington State Bungalow. It is a wood-sided home with a shingle roof that fits quietly under the sheltering

canopy of tall fir trees. Peeking out from behind the oversize geometrically patterned gable, reminiscent of Wright's Oak Park home, are the twin stacks of the chimney, serving two fireplaces—this is a house that takes seriously the idea of the hearth as the center of a home. The house is so perfect for both its site and the owner that you would think that Sharon and Ken spent countless hours going over each detail—not that it is a house built from speculative plans.

This Bungalow seems particularly suited to the Northwest region, a part of the country with a heightened awareness of nature and climate. With its soaring ceilings and a palette of grays and golds in the wood, stone, and tile, this house responds to the ephemeral weather changes that continually alter the views. One moment the entire landscape can be enshrouded in wooly fog, and in the next, sunlight makes diamonds out of raindrops.

ABOVE, **The steeply pitched roof** is well suited to climates with abundant rain and snowfall.

FACING PAGE, **A wet bar** is tucked into a corridor between the living room and family room, serving both rooms with ease.

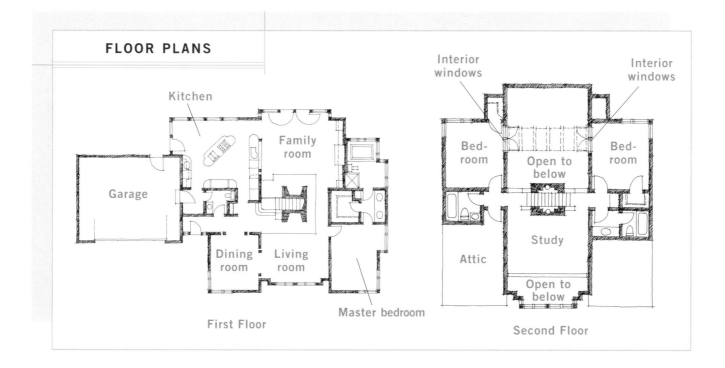

FLOOR PLANS

Kitchen

Family room

Garage

Dining room

Living room

Master bedroom

First Floor

Interior windows

Interior windows

Bed-room

Open to below

Bed-room

Study

Attic

Open to below

Second Floor

High-gloss finishes on wood, chrome, glass, and tile serve to bounce light and to create rooms that look active and vibrant.

Sharon loves the way the clapboard siding picks up the colors of the wooded landscape; she notes that the rough edges of the roof shingles look much like the fissured bark of the surrounding fir trees. From the backyard, particularly, the cascade of roof planes and arbors ties the house to its site.

A phalanx of skylights punctures the roof to capture the fleeting sunlight, and the Bungalow demonstrates just how important windows can be to an overall design, both in their selection and in their placement. Viewed from the backyard, the wall above the major living area has no windows; instead, the second-story windows are pushed back to make them less noticeable, with the effect of playing down the full height of the house.

Windows also have been placed in the interior walls of the two upstairs bedrooms, opening into the double-height living room. In this way, the living room func-

Every Bungalow is a little idiosyncratic: As a whimsical touch, several sections of white oak flooring have been interspersed with the red oak.

ABOVE, **The interior window** of this bedroom provides cross-ventilation, takes advantage of illumination from the skylights, and allows the cook to call upstairs when dinner is ready.

FACING PAGE, **Early Bungalows** often employed the device of hanging a large mirror over the mantel to make the room appear twice its actual size. But this is not an optical illusion here; this Bungalow has twin fireplaces.

tions something like a town square. Sharon's guests can poke their heads out of the bedrooms and join in the conversation below. In addition to being a novelty, this serves to improve the ventilation, often a challenge with a Bungalow's second-story bedrooms. The living room is also overlooked by a small loft above the area, and the wide, carpeted steps might easily double as the hub of a party.

Warming Up the Interior

The honey tones of Douglas fir molding and wide-plank red oak floors add warmth to the white walls and the grays of the tiles. The stair, with its chrome railing and cutouts in the flanking walls, takes center stage as it ascends between the twin fireplaces.

Prairie Craftsman Bungalow

FOR MANY PEOPLE, an American Prairie Craftsman Bungalow may describe one very nice house, or two styles and one home, or best of all a splendid lifestyle.

All born at the end of the 19th century, these sibling styles and building typologies were made possible by the American emergence of individuality, confidence, and economic opportunity.

Wisconsin-bred Frank Lloyd Wright is credited with developing the Prairie style of architecture,

where small- and low-scale residential or commercial buildings used materials, trim, and ornamentation to emphasize their horizontality in order to relate to their site and surroundings. Wisconsin-bred Gustav Stickley, through his widely read magazine *The Craftsman,* sang the praises of handcrafted furniture, housing, and natural lifestyle—a notion derived from the Arts and Crafts Movement, begun by Englishman William Morris.

Marching from the East and the West coasts at about the same time, the Bungalow was introduced and enjoyed wide popularity among those partaking of the American economic dream. The Bungalow is a housing type but not specifically a visual or aesthetic style like Prairie or Craftsman.

Some of the finer and more familiar Bungalow examples are those realized in a Craftsman or Prairie or even Prairie Craftsman style.

There is a horizontal banding of wood trim high on the walls, but it does not define the line between wall and ceiling in the manner of crown molding. Instead, this strip has a unifying function, tying together the built-ins and vertical trim to give these rooms a more cohesive horizontal feeling.

Just as in many early Bungalows, one bedroom in Sharon's home is on the first floor. This is hardly the tiny bedroom of the past, but a luxurious suite with as much attention to tilework and woodwork as in the living area. The Jacuzzi® tub offers a 90-degree view of the wooded landscape beyond. Even though the suite is on the first floor, its triangulated ceiling recalls the quirky geometry of old Bungalow bedrooms under the eaves, with the same comforting sense of cocooning.

In early Bungalows, the entertainment system consisted of an upright piano and a few harmonizing voices.

Today, new homes often have to accommodate wall-size entertainment systems, and unless these systems are considered from the beginning of design, they can dominate what was meant to be a family space. In this living room, Ken devoted a special niche in the built-in bookcase to the large-screen television. The room, with its unobtrusive low-voltage lighting system, emphasizes the large glazed-tile fireplace and hearth by night; during the day, the eye is drawn to the views through the soaring windows.

The dining room is slightly set off from the rest of the house by a framed opening, an exercise in simplicity that calls to mind the Japanese influence on Frank Lloyd Wright. The restrained palette of materials, red oak flooring, a corner window for panoramic views, and a coved ceiling trimmed in Douglas fir all work to create a restorative feeling, perfect for companionship and conversation.

LEFT, **Views of the distant landscape** can have a restorative effect on the mind. Bottom-up shades are an elegant way of providing as much view (or as much privacy) as the bather desires.

FACING PAGE, **Framing and trim** have been used as an architectural device throughout this house, unifying the rooms into a coherent whole.

Traditional Lines, Modern Materials

ABOVE, **Combinations of brick, wood,** stucco, and stone are common in historic Bungalow construction. The lesson was not lost on this brand-new Bungalow.

FACING PAGE, **The overhanging balcony** sets the stage for a dramatic preview of the activities in the living room below.

T AKE A CLOSE LOOK AT THIS IOWA BUNGALOW. It isn't quite what it seems. This area of the Midwest has a tradition of building with local materials, particularly a quarried limestone that is ideal for homes, retaining walls, and patios, but this design draws on radically recycled materials in expressing a familiar style.

The limestone is actually a composite of pulverized quarry stone, rubber, and colorants, formed to look like natural rock. The wood siding is a new product, comprised of wood fibers and Portland cement. And the slate roof? Another innovation, combining finely crushed slate rubble and polymer resin binders. The house was framed with wood from sustainable forests, grown specifically for the building industry and carefully replanted. The owner and builder, Ralph, can take satisfaction in knowing that his house places less of a burden on resources than conventional construction.

A Modest Appearance

At almost 5,000 sq. ft., Ralph and Diane's Bungalow could hardly be called a modest home, but in keeping with the style, it strives to put forth a modest aspect from the front yard. Who would guess that this seem-

LEFT, **The balcony serves** as a conversation nook as well as a desk for school papers or letter writing. Family members don't have to retreat to their rooms when they need a little peace and quiet to do their work.

FACING PAGE, **The overhanging** balconies create a low ceiling over the seating area, for an intimate setting for conversation, with a dramatic view to the landscape.

ABOVE, **Only from the privacy** of the backyard are the full three stories of the house evident. The architect took advantage of this sloped site to design a house that is much bigger than it looks from the street.

ingly one-story house has three full floors of living space? The subtle layering of roof planes and the gentle easing of the house into the slope make it appear smaller, as does the horizontal effect of the siding and masonry.

Architect Ken Dahlin uses the Prairie feature of the vaulted ceiling, emphasized here with doubled wood banding. This design device resembles a beam from the double-height living room, and it looks more like pure decoration when viewed from the loft space, where the vault is less dramatic than it is cozy and encompassing. The vault is played up by concealed low-voltage lighting, set on a dimmer to adjust the light level to suit the activity.

Although this is a good-size house, the bedrooms are relatively small, with the effect of encouraging Ralph's family to gravitate to the shared rooms for projects, homework, and reading. As with Bungalows of the past,

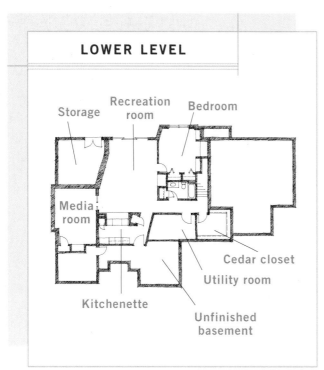

LOWER LEVEL

Storage

Recreation room

Bedroom

Media room

Kitchenette

Utility room

Cedar closet

Unfinished basement

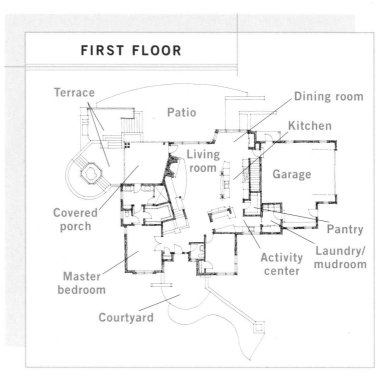

FIRST FLOOR

Terrace

Patio

Dining room

Kitchen

Living room

Garage

Covered porch

Pantry

Activity center

Laundry/ mudroom

Master bedroom

Courtyard

SECOND FLOOR

Loft/study

Open to below

Bedroom

Study

Bed-room

Bed-room

this floor plan contributes in a subtle way to family togetherness. Even with the open plan, there are places to be "away" while still being together—the loft, the computer station, and the dining room. The kitchen was designed for family cooking and family eating. The cabinets are constructed of another new material: panels of white straw fibers and resin glues. The banquette conceals the sink, dishwasher, and second oven from the view of the family room.

Not Your Basic Basement

Unlike the behemoth multiarmed furnaces in musty old Bungalow basements, the only frightening things apt to appear in this lower level of the house are on the screen in the media room. The architect was able to take advantage of the grade's slope down to the back-

ABOVE, **Kitchens today** are a central part of family living and often flow into other rooms. This kitchen pulls out all the stops. The built-in dining counter is the closest thing to a shrine for eating that we have seen. The joinery recalls early Craftsman carpentry techniques.

RIGHT, **In original Bungalows,** art glass, fine tile-work, and elaborate woodwork were reserved for the formal living and dining spaces. In this new bathroom, improved finishes allow the use of varnished wood without worrying about the effects of humidity.

yard, allowing the recreation room and its kitchenette to open out directly to the patio. Even a lower level, if well designed, can enjoy the benefits of daylight. The key to success is providing enough window area in relation to the floor area.

Thanks in large part to generous windows and easy outdoor access, this level is not the sort of place where kids traditionally were banished to get them out of sight and out of mind. In fact, kids and adults are apt to squabble good naturedly over whose turn it is to entertain there.

ABOVE, **This multipurpose room** enjoys plenty of daylight and easy access to the spacious yard. A collection of game boards is displayed on the plate rail.

FACING PAGE, **Translucent glass** in the double doors provides privacy while brightening up what could be a dark hallway.

In the
Newport Tradition

Bungalows favor the use of natural material, with full knowledge that maintenance will be a necessity. Shingles advertise their age and the effects of weathering, becoming increasingly attractive over the years.

Shingle style ⌐ A New England–based style of the late 1800s, characterized by a hipped roof, a wide porch, an asymmetrical form, and shingled walls and roofing.

A S WITH MANY OLDER BUNGALOWS, THIS ONE IN Jamestown, Rhode Island, was influenced by regional architecture. Designed for a developer by the architectural firm of Estes/Twombly, it borrows the New England **Shingle style's** hipped roof and characteristic siding. The house is deceptively small. When we reviewed photos of the project for inclusion in this book, we thought the scale on the plans had to be wrong. This grand house couldn't possibly fit on only a sixth of an acre! In fact, the area of the first floor is just 900 sq. ft.

The house's composition is in the form of two boxes, linked by 620 sq. ft. of covered veranda. Add 500 finished sq. ft. on the second floor and another 300 sq. ft. over the garage, and the result is just a tad above the national average. But the living space looks (and acts) like so much more.

Shingles and Shadows

The careful design adds visual interest through rhythm, repetition, and restraint. Outside, the palette of materials is simple, drawing on cedar shingles for the walls and dark green trim for the doors, windows, columns, and fascia boards. The shingles, a common siding on New

The bridgelike veranda acts both as a place for the family to relax and a welcoming area to greet clients before getting down to business in the office over the garage.

Traditionally, Bungalows have embraced local materials and regional styles. This new Rhode Island Bungalow borrows from New England's distinctive Shingle style.

England homes, have a thick cut that casts a textured shadow, emphasizing the low Bungalow profile. The deep overhang casts its shadow as well, helping to visually trim down the height of the walls.

Inside, the stone fireplace, beams, and pine flooring and paneling all give the house a hearty, somewhat rough-hewn feeling. The living and dining rooms and the kitchen pivot around the centrally located hearth. A small but efficient planning area is built into the back of the fireplace wall; it's a quiet space, just in view of major comings and goings but handy enough to serve as the home's nerve center.

Upstairs, shed dormers do a remarkable job of turning the space under that low hipped roof into sunny, attractive rooms. Unlike the convention followed by many Bungalows, these dormers do not introduce a contrast of color or materials to the overall design but make use of the shingles and painted trim found elsewhere.

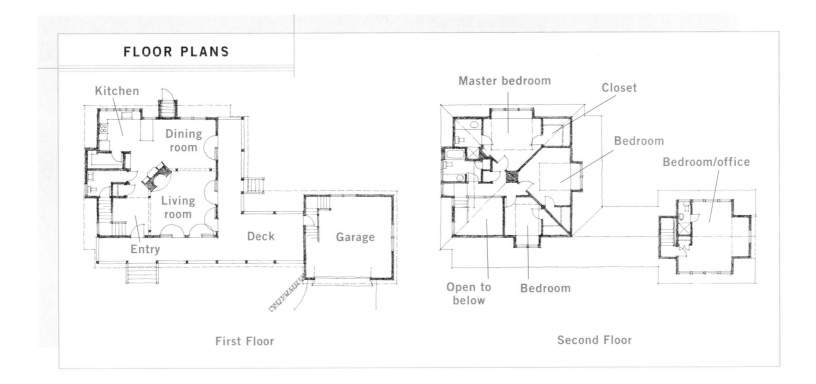

FLOOR PLANS

Kitchen

Dining room

Living room

Entry

Deck

Garage

First Floor

Master bedroom

Closet

Bedroom

Bedroom/office

Open to below

Bedroom

Second Floor

A Year-Round Veranda

The portion of the veranda that links the house and garage is glazed, allowing the family to use it in all kinds of weather. The owners chose to work from the home, and their office is above the garage; their short commute is a pleasant one, with views along either side of the veranda as they leave the house. The large awning windows in the office's dormers make this space far more gracious than a glimpse from the exterior would suggest.

Verandas are useful as flexible space. They expand the usable living area of the house because they aren't specifically programmed for one function. If adapted with screens, they are more pleasant in summer. And by installing windows, as with this house, a sunny veranda may trap enough heat to be enjoyed on winter days. You'll also be able to use something other

The roof is the unifying element of this architectural composition, tying together the house, the garage (with its office above), and the veranda that links them.

At the hub of this house, a storage wall acts as command central, with the phone, calendar, and school permission slips easily at hand.

than outdoor furniture there, making the area all the more welcoming.

This home is another example of how long-standing ideas about shelter and comfort can continue to shape today's architecture. Although the design is a departure from tradition, it was arrived at through a familiarity with the traditions of the Bungalow and Shingle styles, as well as with the region's own particular architectural history. This is the challenge in arriving at a home you'll love—adapting time-tested floor plans, materials, and detailing in a way that will be both familiar and invigorating, both cozy and practical. The Bungalow, with its common sense and flexibility, continues to be an excellent theme on which to improvise in your own fashion.

Floor Show

FITTING IN

☆

WHEN BUILDING a new Bungalow, one of the most important and long-lasting decisions you will make is the choice of flooring material. During the first wave of Bungalow building, tongue-and-groove floors were standard—typically, oak or maple in the formal rooms and pine or a lesser grade of maple in the bedrooms. These floors are durable and attractive and can stand up to being refinished a number of times. In a subtle way, they establish a link with the Bungalow's heritage. All of that solid wood costs a good deal, however, and there is also the labor involved in putting down the many pieces.

A fairly recent alternative is a composite wood floor, with a veneer of hardwood over a substrate of a less expensive species. These floors offer wood for less cost, but the relatively thin top layer can't be sanded down as many times. A new kid on the block is a vinyl flooring that features a photographic impression of wood. These floors look like the real thing, and they are easy to clean. Instead, you might prefer a retro vinyl floor that mimics the linoleum patterns used in old Bungalow kitchens. Enjoying great popularity today is the laminate floor that employs a coated plastic laminate (like your countertops) bonded to a flooring substrate.

The front door of this home opens on a two-story space. That often creates a formal feeling in a traditional home, but the open plan of this new Rhode Island home reflects a family-friendly house that does not stand on ceremony.

Historic Housing

ABOVE, **One common complaint** about new construction is that it lacks the detail that makes older houses so interesting. This Bungalow has elephant columns (so-called because of their resemblance to elephant's legs) with corner trim, bricks that look convincingly old, wood siding, and art glass in the door.

FACING PAGE, **While this house** does not have a true double-front gable, the lattice provides an ornament reminiscent of details commonly found on older Bungalows. The delightful shadow play changes the appearance of the front of the Bungalow throughout the day.

SPRECKELS IS A SMALL TOWN IN CALIFORNIA'S Salinas Valley, named after Claus Spreckels, a sugar-beet magnate. Between 1900 and 1930, a large collection of Bungalows was built for the managers of his sugar-beet refinery. Bungalows were very popular in company towns throughout America, from Standard Oil in Illinois to Bethlehem Steel in Pennsylvania. The style was favored because it was spacious, easy to construct, and simple to modify—one plan could be repeated with minor exterior modifications for the sake of variety.

Today, the town of Spreckels is designated as a historic district for its intact representation of early 1900s' Bungalow worker housing. While it is great to live in a community rich with history, building a new house within the restrictions of the setting can be a challenge. When a contractor contacted architect Thomas Carleton about designing speculative homes, Tom was faced with tough criteria. First, the contractor required that the houses have twice the square footage of the historic Bungalows and include contemporary interiors that were open in plan, with high ceilings and up-to-date kitchens. Construction costs? The budget allowed

The new Bungalows in Spreckels, California, follow the tone set by the original Bungalows. They are designed for middle-class living: They fit right in with the rhythmical rise and fall of the neighboring rooflines.

historic review board ⌐ A board that reviews alterations and new construction for compatability to historic districts.

less than $100 per square foot. This per-square-foot budget was so low that most architects would have thrown up their hands and walked away from the challenge. In addition, to win the approval of the county's **historic review board,** the new designs had to match the older homes in terms of style, exterior colors and details, roof pitch, and building materials—no vinyl siding and no stone.

Tom did it all and won awards in the process, testifying that his creative interpretation of the historic Bungalow style was successful. "Interpretation" often is an important word when building in a historic setting. New construction typically mimics tradition, but a more satisfying alternative can be to acknowledge and even accentuate the differences. For example, Tom exaggerated several Bungalow elements, such as the taper in the columns, the overlapping roofs, and certain decorative wood elements. He employed wood grills to give a delightful sense of a double gable without actual-

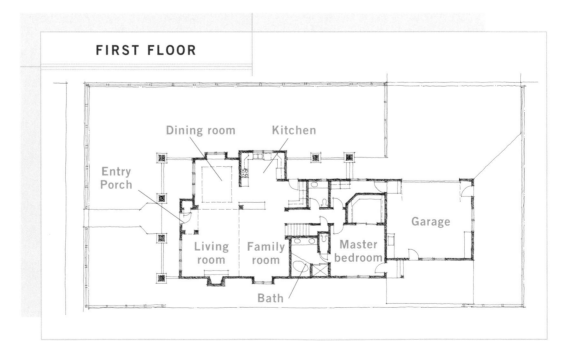

FIRST FLOOR

Dining room   Kitchen

Entry Porch

Garage

Living room   Family room   Master bedroom

Bath

Light and bright, open and airy, the interiors of the Spreckels Bungalows are a break from the tradition of dark woodwork and extensive built-ins.

ly having two gables as structural elements. It is clear to anyone visiting the neighborhood which ones are the old houses and which are the new. Tom's designs are not pale imitations but new creations, to be appreciated in their own right.

Anatomy of a Spec House

Buying a speculative house from a developer allows you to own a new home without the countless decisions involved in finding a lot, working with a design professional, or coming up with your own plans.

As is often true of spec houses, the price for these Bungalows was kept down, in part, by spending money where it was most noticeable—quality materials were used on the exterior. Like original Bungalows, these new Bungalows have wood siding and shingles, masonry chimneys, decorative wood elements, wood columns with masonry bases, and double-hung wood windows—all of them standard. As is common practice in speculative housing (even in original 1920s' Bungalow subdivisions), a basic plan was varied from house to house by flipping the entry or switching from a shed dormer to a

gable. The materials were changed as well. Each of the new Spreckels houses differs in the type of brick for its masonry, the style of column, and the color scheme. Typically, when cost cutting comes to the fore, variety in materials is one of the first things dropped—and it shows. A strong review board, like the one in Spreckels, can ensure that this will not happen.

The interiors are airy, open, and more contemporary than the conventional image of a Bungalow. This was the intention, Tom said: "It's a flip from the outside appearance." And the homeowners still have plenty of opportunity to make these rooms truly their own. If we come back in five years, we might find that wood trim and built-ins have been added, among other traditional features. Or, it could be that the owners continue to appreciate the contrast between the traditional streetscape and the up-to-date interiors. As the Spreckels houses help introduce Bungalows to another generation, it will be interesting to see how the style continues to evolve.

ABOVE, **In some communities,** design restrictions can impart a sense of falseness to new construction. Faux Tudors, Colonials, and Mediterraneans—constructed of synthetic materials—clash with older homes of brick, stone, and wood. Spreckels wisely required that new homes use similar materials to those found on existing Bungalows.

RIGHT, **Traditional porches** have disappeared from most houses today, in favor of decks. These new homes have the Bungalow's distinctive recessed porch, a shaded haven for hot summer days.

Dormer Transformations

A DORMER can be thought of as an architectural device that helps to colonize a cramped second floor under a low roof. It provides light and headroom, while breaking up the large expanse of roof. Because dormers are a traditional way of exploiting the second floor of a Bungalow, you can think of them as one type of addition that will make the house look truer to the style.

A dormer should take its design cues, in terms of both detailing and materials, from the rest of the home, although you may want to scale down braces and other elements. All of this isn't to say that

a dormer has to be merely a little clone of the house below. It can introduce accents of color or details not found elsewhere in the facade.

Bungalows usually have either **shed dormers** or **gable dormers,** classified by their roof types. The roof of a **hipped dormer** has a third, outward facing pitch, or "hip." An **engaged gable dormer** extends to the edge of the roof, and rises up from the eave or wall below.

Dormers vary in both their width (up to the full width of the house) and their depth (at the deepest, from the ridge of the home's roof to its eave). An architect can help you

visualize how much space and headroom you'll gain with various types and sizes. It helps to see a cutaway view with figures and furniture drawn in for a sense of scale, although even the most sophisticated drawings can't convey the effect that daylight, fresh air, and elbow room will have on a cramped attic. Dormers are structural additions, and both their framing and the weight they transfer to the house must be considered carefully. Unless you are experienced in construction, consult with a contractor or architect before opening your roof to the sky.

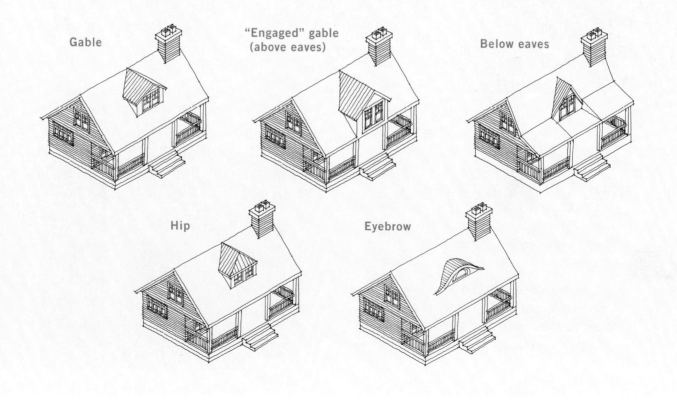

Gable

"Engaged" gable (above eaves)

Below eaves

Hip

Eyebrow

CHAPTER FIVE

THE ONCE AND FUTURE BUNGALOW

ABOVE, **Ornamented windows** are a Bungalow hallmark. These contemporary "off the shelf" windows create soaring space in an attic conversion.

FACING PAGE, **This bedroom** calls to mind the popular Japanese transforming toy, which changes from a robot into a car with a flick of the wrist. In much the same way, the walls of this room can be transformed completely.

W HAT WILL THE BUNGALOW OF THE FUTURE look like? It may have already arrived and it may be in your neighborhood. Brazen new innovations in building materials and forms have quietly slipped into older neighborhoods. Geoff Warner, his wife Dawn, and their kids live in a 1925 Bungalow in a Minneapolis Bungalow neighborhood that, at first glance, looks very ordinary. It takes a closer look to see hints that this Bungalow is different from its neighboring Bungalows. For starters, tucked behind a conventional double fronted gable is a shark's fin of corrugated metal siding, arching back toward the ridge of the roof. On the other side of the roof, a small porthole window winks at the passerby.

Geoff is the architect of a project showcased earlier in this book (see pp. 66–69), but this time he has gotten a little bolder and has had a little more fun. You may wonder how an addition constructed of bent and twisted metal and glass can be compatible with a 1920s Bunga-

ABOVE, **While most people** want to live in a house with up-to-date appliances, few of us would care to have bold, new technologies mounted on the facades of our homes. This house has its futuristic elements, but they aren't obvious from the street.

low. As we enter the new century, building materials that had been reserved for the avant-garde are now commonplace in remodeling and new construction. Architects today are interested in spaces that are warped, rippled, collapsed, bent, and twisted. And they have the computer programs capable of rendering the spaces in a way that previously was very difficult to communicate.

New materials are lighter, and their capacity to span long distances with fewer vertical supports can free us from the box (mentally and physically!). Even an ordinary material like drywall can now be bent to form curves and vaults. By removing extraneous walls and opening up the ceiling, many of the common complaints about the second floor of the Bungalow—poor ventilation, dim illumination, and inadequate headroom—can be remedied. All of these changes can be made while maintaining the cohesive and comforting streetscape of Bungalow neighborhoods.

Geoff and Dawn always knew they would do something with their house, especially with the two small and uninteresting rooms on the second floor. The remodel naturally evolved as he and Dawn thought about how their family lives and what kind of spaces they enjoy. The couple likes to cook, eat, and spend time with their kids. They wanted a home office, they didn't want to spend a lot of money, and they wanted their home to express fine finishes and a high standard of craftsmanship.

In addition to being an architect, Geoff has construction experience, and he occasionally gets the opportunity to actually build part of his projects as a break from sitting behind a computer. He has learned that when you open up a wall of an older home, you should anticipate some surprises, such as unexplained substitutions in building materials or a gap in the spacing of key structural members. Instead of being daunted by these mysteries, Geoff sees them as challenges that require creative solutions.

Innovation in the Kitchen

Like many homeowners, the first projects Dawn and Geoff tackled were floor refinishing and a kitchen remodel. The first floor of their Bungalow looks fairly traditional. The wood floors have a natural finish that contrasts nicely with the dark varnish of the door, three-over-one window frames, and built-in cupboards. The molding around the ceiling is painted white to help make the ceilings feel higher than they actually are.

Original Bungalow kitchens have their charm, but they are much smaller and less well appointed than the kitchens most of us want. Many Bungalow owners decide the kitchen is one place where a total makeover is justified. But Geoff and Dawn decided to make the most of the existing kitchen, infusing it with new features. The kitchen is not all homey and homely; daring

The second floor was reworked to give the feeling of opposition, compression, and expansion, which creates the suspense you might experience walking down a winding alley. This novel approach to space is reinforced by the odd matchup of materials.

If you can't change the footprint of your kitchen, consider going straight up. By raising the ceiling of this kitchen, the room appears larger even though the square footage remains the same.

and whimsical elements of design were added. To set the tone, Geoff knocked out the ceiling, added a skylight, and exposed the joists, which he promptly painted silver.

Dawn and Geoff created additional kitchen work space by recycling an old drafting table. Its wooden top and cast-iron supports fit right in with the eclectic palette of recycled and new materials. Under a lowered ceiling rests a small booth that not only recalls Midwest diners but is also the perfect size from which to oversee the children's latest project while preparing a meal. It is also a cozy place for the family to enjoy a cup of hot chocolate and watch the snow swirl beyond the ornamented windows.

Making functional objects from found objects is one of Geoff's specialties. A professional cook's rack is an expensive item, so Geoff fashioned his own from off-the-shelf items from a local hardware store and secured the rack to the beams with rope and fancy knots. This contraption is illuminated by another Warner exclusive, the colander light fixture, which shoots starlike beams of light over the pots and pans. With a nod to Bungalow tradition, the art-glass windows add a touch of elegance to the kitchen.

Whimsy in the Bathroom

The first-floor bathroom continues the theme of retaining the charming elements of the original Bungalow while adding humor and illusion. Wood trim pieces surround the medicine cabinet mirror and the window next to the old cast-iron tub. The wood trim on the wall acts as a transition piece between classic square white tiles and the painted upper wall. The sculptural metal showerhead, the shower and curtain rod of cop-

As with the rest of the house, this bathroom blends the expected with the brash and innovative. The shower plumbing and curtain rod are sketched in ordinary copper supply tubing.

Think Reuse

FITTING IN

☆ **ANYONE WHO HAS EVER** remodeled a kitchen knows that kitchen cabinets are a large part of the budget. The original cabinets in most Bungalow kitchens were constructed of solid wood. More often than not, some part of the original cabinets have been refinished and retained in previous renovations. Even if the hardware has to be replaced, period reproductions are easy to find now with the proliferation of Bungalow products on the market.

per tubing, the stainless-steel sink, and a pullout shaving mirror all combine to make this bathroom a prime example of invention and tradition. A lamp that strangely resembles an old-fashioned girdle sheds diffuse light over the composition.

Drama in the Attic

Two small bedrooms comprised the upstairs of the Warner Bungalow, and one was used as a home office. Sleeping there was not very romantic and working there was uninspired. By making use of every square inch of unused attic space and lots of creative thinking, Geoff and Dawn gained an additional 200 sq. ft. of living space. The second floor of their Bungalow was transformed into a bedroom/office suite that would be the envy of many an urban loft dweller.

Mention drywall as a building material, and most people conjure up images of bland, boxy rooms with little drama. Now, thanks to new flexible studs, drywall can be formed into curving walls, much faster and less expensively than plaster walls.

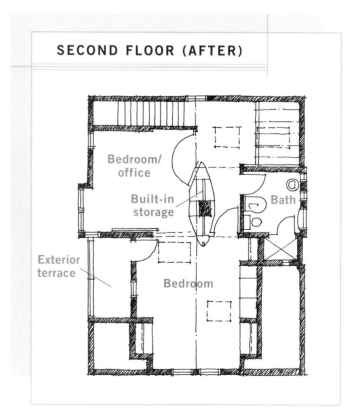

SECOND FLOOR (AFTER)

Bedroom/office

Built-in storage

Bath

Exterior terrace

Bedroom

Geoff realized the potential hidden in the volume of the Bungalow roof to create dramatic space and used some dynamic construction techniques to express it. Wherever possible, Geoff took out the ceiling and extended the vertical space of the second story all the way to the ridgeline of the roof. Not content with merely going up, he bent and curved the walls to give the impression that the rooms are sculpted space, not constructed space. The walls feel (and are) thicker. The second floor gives the impression of a grand space hovering in the sky, not a warren of small dark rooms tucked under a low roof.

Not only is the space sculptural, but it is kinetic. Geoff designed and built oversize metal doors to slide out from a pocket and become a movable wall between the bedroom and the office. He also created a floor-to-ceiling structure that is both wall and ceiling. Recycled industrial wooden pallets, those wooden platforms used in shipping, slide up and down a metal armature to create wood wainscoting in the down position, hiding closet and dresser drawers. In the up position, the ceiling takes on the appearance of wood decking. The pal-

Be It Ever So Industrial...

EARLY BUNGALOW DESIGNERS made use of locally available construction materials to save money and time, and as a result these houses took on a character that was true to their roots and sensibilities. Today, when homes like the one in this chapter draw on sturdy, low-cost industrial products, innovative materials, and reclaimed objects, they express a new aesthetic that is both practical and contemporary. For example, concrete has become a popular choice for countertops and kitchen floors, copper and terne is used as exterior siding, and marine plywood is specified for flooring. In the hands of a sensitive, confident architect or homeowner, the effect can still feel like your home rather than a noble experiment.

If you live in an aesthetically conservative community, this sort of design might be a tough sell. Look for precedents of modern remodeling in your community.

ABOVE, **These handcrafted** rubber cabinet pulls fit in with the impromptu spirit of the bedroom's pallet-wood cabinetry.

FACING PAGE, **The family calls** this wheeled contraption the Trojan sink, after the soldier-filled horse on wheels used to attack ancient Troy, but in fact the sink is anchored quite securely in place. Towels are hung over the wall-mounted radiator so that they'll be toasty on winter mornings.

lets are used again to form a storage wall for books between the bedroom and the office. The scale of the wood is a play on expensive paneling, and the curve of the wall adds to the mystery of what exactly is the shape of these rooms. The shape continually changes depending on what activity is taking place.

The color scheme was chosen for its timelessness. The exposed joists are clad in sheet metal, and the bed frame is painted a silvery tone. Both reflect the machine aesthetic of the building materials and the continually changing atmospheric effect of light and shadow patterns. The dappled effect of the blue rag-painted wall heightens the sense that the room is up in the clouds.

Minneapolis has more sunny winter days than almost any other northern city in the United States. The many and varied windows in the second-floor remodeling take full advantage of this delightful natural phenomenon. Even the second-floor bathroom sneaks in two small windows on either side of the sink that not only bring in morning sun but also double as display spaces for well-designed toiletries (see the photo on the facing page). The sink, called the Trojan sink by the family, acts as centerpiece. It's mounted on serious-looking rubber wheels but in fact is securely anchored to the floor.

You might think that with all of these moving parts and recycled machinelike pieces that the remodel would be a cold and dizzying space to be in. But Geoff says the family enjoys being high above everyone else and closer to the sky than to the ground. To this end, he designed a small terrace for his family to enjoy. Sandwiched between two dormers for privacy, the family can sit outside and read bedtime stories catching the

Second-floor sleeping porches were once a common feature on Bungalows. This house has a second-floor *sitting* porch, and it seems more like a perch with its view of the street. The porch is recessed below the roof pitch and doesn't advertise its presence to passersby.

last bit of the warmth of the sun reflected off the galvanized metal roof. The overall effect of the remodel is not all hardware and recycled materials but one of a refined space that is rich in detail and finishes. In this project, the whole is bigger than the sum of its parts—a difficult thing to achieve if there isn't a big design idea behind all the nifty materials.

The Warner Bungalow is an excellent example of the Bungalow of the future. It clearly employs the inventiveness of necessity, celebrating the way people live today without taking itself too seriously. As Geoff says, you don't need to live in a huge house; you need to enjoy inhabiting more of the space you already have.

With One Foot in the Past, Bungalows Gallop into the Future

In gathering information for this book we were struck by the affection people have for the Bungalow style, even if they have never lived in a Bungalow. To most people, the Bungalow expresses what is right about housing.

The Bungalow is ubiquitous: Everyone knows someone who has lived in a Bungalow. When someone new comes into our home, they always have a Bungalow story to tell. They mention the built-ins, the oddly shaped ceilings, and the beautiful woodwork, but most of all, they describe how at home the house makes

Back to the Beginning

GEOFF WARNER is not howling alone in the wilderness with his new take on the Bungalow. In California, Linnea and John began with this 1923 Bungalow, a tight budget, and a clear design direction for their remodeling (she is a clothing designer and he is an animation artist). They wanted to entertain, show off their art collection, and have the house reflect their industrial aesthetic. With the help of the Sintesi design group, sheet metal, concrete, plastic, galvanized metal, and found objects were transformed into recognizable features—floors, cabinets, and counters. By cutting holes in ceilings, designing with light and shadow, and using more inventiveness than money, the four collaborators turned something of a caterpillar into a butterfly.

them feel and how much they enjoy the companionable Bungalow neighborhoods.

For over 100 years, the Bungalow style has delivered the goods on the promises the original Bungalow advertisers made: affordable housing with high-quality construction that encourages family togetherness and connectedness to the community.

Bungalow mania was made possible because the style was flexible enough to suit almost anyone's aesthetic, yet the hallmarks were so well defined that the style had great integrity. These are exactly the qualities that excite homeowners in this new century about the possibilities of building new Bungalows, breathing life into aging Bungalows, and restoring classic Bungalows.

Sources

BOOKS

Bowman, Leslie Greene. *American Arts & Crafts*. Boston: Bulfinch Press, 1990.

Duchscherer, Paul, and Douglas Keister. *The Bungalow*. New York: Penguin Studio, 1995.

King, Anthony D. *The Bungalow: The Production of a Global Culture*. Boston: Routledge Kegan & Paul, 1984.

Lancaster, Clay. *The American Bungalow*. New York: Abbeville Press, 1985.

Makinson, Randell L. *Greene & Greene*. Salt Lake City: Gibbs-Smith, 1998.

Stickley, Gustav. *The Best of Craftsman Homes*. Santa Barbara, Calif., and Salt Lake City: Peregrine Smith, 1979.

Susanka, Sarah. *The Not So Big House*. Newtown, Conn.: The Taunton Press, 1998.

Winter, Robert. *American Bungalow Style*. New York: Simon & Schuster, 1996.

MAGAZINES

American Bungalow
PO Box 756
Sierra Madre, CA 91025

Fine Homebuilding
The Taunton Press
63 S. Main St., PO Box 5506
Newtown CT 06470
(800) 477-8727
www.taunton.com

Historic Preservation
National Trust for Historic Preservation
1785 Massachusetts Ave., NW
Washington, DC 20036
www.nationaltrust.org

Old-House Journal
Dovetail Publishers
2 Main St.
Gloucester, MA 01930
www.oldhousejournal.com

ASSOCIATIONS

Arts and Crafts Materials Institute
715 Boylston St.
Boston, MA 02116

Arts and Crafts Movement Resource Directory
www.ragtime.org

Bungalow Heaven Neighborhood Assoc.
PO Box 40812
Pasadena, CA 91114
www.home.earthlink.net/~bhna

Center for Tapestry Arts
167 Spring St.
New York, NY 10012

Craftsman Home Owners
Roycroft Associates
31 South Grove St.
East Aurora, NY 14052

Historic Chicago Bungalow Assoc.
1 North Lacily St., 12th Floor
Chicago, IL 60602
www.chicagobungalow.org

National Trust for Historic Preservation
1785 Massachusetts Ave., NW
Washington, DC 20036
www.nationaltrust.org

Preservation Assistance Div.
National Park Service
U.S. Dept. of the Interior
PO Box 37127
Washington, DC 20013

Seattle Bungalow and Craftsman Home Fair
Historic Seattle
1117 Minor Ave.
Seattle, WA 98101
www.cityofseattle.net/commnty/histsea/programs/bungalow.htm

Twin Cities Bungalow Club
3547 24th Ave. South
Minneapolis, MN 55406
www.mtn.org/bungalow

FURNISHINGS

Andersen Windows, Inc.
Residential Products
Customer Service Department
1004th Ave. North
Bayport, MN 55003
(800) 426-4261, ext. 2542
www.andersenwindows.com

Aurora Studios
50 Bull Hill Rd.
Woodstock, CT 06281
(860) 928-1963

Bradbury and Bradbury
PO Box 155
Benicia, CA 94510
www.bradbury.com

Brass Light Gallery
131 S. First St.
Milwaukee, WI 53204
www.brasslight.com

The Bright Spot
33 Chestnut Ave.
Westmont, IL 60515
www.thebrightspot.com

J. R. Burrows and Co.
PO Box 522
Rockland, MA 02370

Certainteed Corp.
Sales Support
PO Box 860
Valley Forge, PA 19842
(800) 233-8990
www.certainteed.com

Designs in Tile
PO Box 358
Mount Shasta, CA 96067

Evergreen Studios
6543 Alpine Dr., SW
Olympia, WA 98512
(360) 352-0694

GAF Materials Corp.
1361 Alps Rd.
Wayne, NJ 07470
(800) 766-3411
www.gaf.com

Georgia Pacific Corp.
133 Peachtree St., NE, 8th Floor
Atlanta, GA 30348
(800) 284-5347

Helen Foster Stencils
71 Main St.
Sandford, ME 04073

Johns Manville
717 17th St.
Denver, CO 80217
(800) 654-3103
www.jm.com

Louisiana Pacific Corp.
Specialty Div.
10115 Kincey Ave., Ste. 150
Huntersville, NC 28078
(800) 462-1238
www.lpcorp.com

Maiman Interior Doors
3839 E. Mustard Way
Springfield, MO 65803
(800) 641-4320
www.maiman.com

Marvin Windows and Doors
PO Box 100
Warroad, MN 56763
(888) 819-2470
www.marvin.com

Mica Lamp Co.
517 State St.
Glendale, CA 91203
(818) 241-7227

Mission Spirit
9900 W. Spirit Lake Rd.
Spirit Lake, ID 83869
(800) 433-4211

Moravian Pottery and Tile Works
130 Swamp Rd.
Doylestown, PA 18901
(215) 345-6722

New World Craftsman
1614 Gaylord St.
Denver, CO 80206
(303) 888-9104

Pella Corp.
Residential Products
102 Main St.
Pella, IA 50219
(800) 547-3552
www.pella.com

Rejuvenation Lamp and Fixture Co.
1100 SE Grand Ave.
Portland, OR 97214

Royal Wood
Precision Composites
109 N. 37th Ave., Ste. 1
Phoenix, AZ 85009
www.royal-wood.com

Schlage Hardware
1915 Jamboree Dr.
Colorado Springs, CO 80920
(800) 847-1864
www.schlage.com

Shakertown
PO Box 400
Winlock, WA 98596
(800) 426-8970
www.shakertown.com

L. and J. G. Stickley
PO Box 480
Manlius, NY 13104
www.stickley.com

Tile Showcase
1 Design Center Pl., Ste. 639
Boston, MA 02210
(617) 426-6515

Velux-America
1418 Evans Pond Rd.
Greenwood, SC 29648
(800) 888-3589
www.velux-america.com

Wolverine
750 E. Swedesford Rd.
Valley Forge, PA 19482
(888) 838-8100

HOUSE PLANS
The Bungalow Co.
PO Box 584
Bend, OR 97709
www.tbcompany.com

Homestyles
www.store.homestyles.com

Home Patterns
www.homepatterns.com

HISTORIC PRESERVATION
Association for Preservation Technology
4513 Lincoln Ave., Ste. 213
Lisle, IL 60532
www.apti.org

National Register of Historic Places
www.cr.nps.gov/nr/index.htm

National Trust for Historic Preservation
1785 Massachusetts Ave., NW
Washington, DC 20036
www.nationaltrust.org

ARCHITECTS
American Institute of Architects
www.e-architect.com

Find an Architect/AIA Profile
www.cmdg.com/profile

FEATURED ARCHITECTS

Alchemy
(pp. 36, 42, 43, 45 [left], 49, 51, 52
[top, bottom], 66-69, 186-197)
Geoffrey Warner, Architect
550 Vandalia St. #314
St. Paul, MN 55114
(651) 647-6650
www.alchemyarch.com

Thomas J. Carleton Architecture
(pp. 27 [top, bottom], 139, 180-184)
109 Central Ave.
Salinas, CA 93901
(831) 449-6490
www.tjcaia.com

Caswell Daitch Architects
(pp. 84, 130 [bottom], 132-135)
9604 Bruce Dr.
Silver Spring, MD 20901
(301) 585-8360

Coastline Construction
(pp. v [top], 25, 54-65)
Gary Milici (contractor)
308 NE 59th St.
Seattle, WA 98105
(206) 522-2139
www.coastlineconstruction.com

Paul De Groot, Architect
(pp. 88, 91, 96)
6202 Highland Hills Dr.
Austin, TX 78731
(512) 345-2228

Estes/Twombly Architects
(pp. 138, 174-179)
79 Thames St.
Newport, RI 02840
(401) 846-3336
www.estestwombly.com

Genesis Architecture
(pp. ii, vi, 1 [top], 4, 28 [top], 83, 93, 137, 140, 143,
144, 147, 156-165, 166-173)
Ken Dahlin, Architect
4061 North Main St., Suite 200
Racine, WI 53402-3116
Phone: (262) 752-1894
www.genesisarchitecture.com

Greene and Proppe Design
(pp. 78-83)
Thom Greene, Architect
1209 West Berwyn Ave.
Chicago, IL 60640
(773) 271-1925
www.gpdchicago.com

HSP/Ltd.
(pp. 6, 40, 41, 50, 70-77)
David Seglin, Architect
414 North Orleans #208
Chicago, IL 60610
(312) 467-4700
www.hspltd.com

Jarvis Architects
(pp. 90, 112-117)
5278 College Ave.
Oakland, CA 94618
(510) 654-6755
www.jarvisarchitects.com

Christopher Lynch Architects
(p. 89)
145 Keller St.
Petaluma, CA 94952
(707) 776-0885

Morris-Day Designers and Builders
(pp. v [bottom], 5, 7 [left], 11, 16, 19, 24 [bottom],
95, 97 [top]118-123, 124-131)
Dwight McNeil, Architect
4600-C Lee Hwy.
Arlington, VA 22207
(703) 524-5220
www.morris-day.com

Myefski Cook Architects
(p. 28 [bottom])
716 Vernon Ave.
Glencoe, IL 60022
(847) 835-7081
www.myefskicook.com

Quorum Architects
(pp. iii, 8, 9, 15, 29-35, 97 [bottom])
Allyson Nemec, Architect
3112 West Highland Blvd.
Milwaukee, WI 53208
(414) 265-9265
www.quorumarchitects.com

Sintesi
(p. 197)
3111 4th St. #119
Santa Monica, CA 90405
(310) 452-0073
www.sintesidesign.com

Index

Note: Page references in italics indicate a photograph; page references in bold indicate a drawing; bolded terms indicate a definition.

A

Additions
  eclectic changes to consider, 106, *106, 107, 108,* 109, **109,** 110, *110, 111*
  gaining space by going up, 124, *124, 125,* **126,** 127, **127,** *128,* 129, *129,* 130, *130,* 131, *131*
  layering of spaces, 100, **100,** *101,* 102, *102,* 103, *103, 104*
  merging the old with, 105, *105*
  raising the roof for more space, 105
  reasons for adding on, 87, *87,* 88, *88,* 89, *126*
  stepping back the addition, *84*
Affair at the Bungalow, The (Christie), 16
American Institute of Architects (AIA), 39
Art Deco, 56
Arts and Crafts, 18, 21, 24, 156
Attics
  collar ties in, 52, *52*
  gaining floor space in, 48, **48**
  use of space, 192, *192,* 193

B

Balcony addition, *91*
Bangala, 16, 17
Basements, 62, 64
Bathrooms
  changes in bathroom spaces, *65, 68, 131*
  today's preferences in, *45, 65, 67, 68, 117, 131, 155, 164, 171, 191, 195*
Beaded board, 49
Box beams, 114
Breakfast nook, *60,* 61, **61**
Bungalow, The: The Production of a Global Culture (King), 16–17
Bungalows
  adaptability of style, 12, **12,** 22
  adding on to the home, 26
  appeal as an ideal American home, 6–7, 7, 8, **8,** *9,* 10, **10**
  bangalas in India, 16, 17
  changing the exterior, 28, *28*
  exterior features of, 10, **10,** *54, 55*
  fitting in new construction, *14*
  hallmarks, 10, **10,** 11, *11,* 12, **12,** 13, *13,* 14, **14,** *15,* 16, *16,* 146
  history, 16–17, *17,* 18, *18, 19,* 20, *20*
  marketing, 18, *19,* 20, *21*
  materials for, 174, *174,* 176, *176*
  neighborhoods, 12
  options for, 21–28
  partial walls in, 14, *15*
  period lighting in, 17, *17, 58*
  porches as integral parts of, *8, 9, 19*
  restoration of, 24–25, *25,* 26, *26*
  styles of, 21
  traditional home and traditional design, 11–12
  variations of, **8**
  wall treatments for, 24, *24*
  working within the existing form, 22–23, *23*
  See also Bungalows by location
Bungalows, new, 26, *27*
  reasons to build new, 138, *138,* 139, *139,* 140, *140*
  designing, 143–44, *145*
  finding a lot and identifying future development, 144–45, 146
  working with the view, *148,* 151, *151,* 153

C

Cabinets, built-in, *28*
California Bungalow
  restoring warmth in, 112, *112, 113,* 114, *114, 115,* 116, *116,* 117, *117*
  using local materials in, *115*
Casements, 59, *80, 114*
Casita, 155
Chicago Bungalow, 11
  bricks in, *6*
  transforming the kitchen space of, 78, *78, 79,* **80,** 81, **81,** *82, 83, 83*
Colors, exterior, *52, 113,* 117
Columns, elephant-leg, 29, *180*
Comprehensive plan, 146
Craftsman Bungalows, 24, 26, 36, 56, 57
Craftsmanship, and Bungalows, 56, *136*

D

Dentils, *107,* 110
Doors
  Bungalow-style, 152, **152**
  pocket doors, 102, *192*
  salvaged French doors, 7
Dormers, *5, 11*
  in Bungalow roofs, *112*
  creating a dormer niche, *51*
  gable dormers, 185, **185**
  hipped dormer, 185, **185**
  shed dormers, 185, **185**
Double-gabled, 124
Double-hung, 34
Drywall, 25

F

Fireplaces
  in living rooms, *22, 25,* 74, *75, 102,* 130, *130, 143*
  refacing, 74, *75*
Floors/flooring
  choice of, 178
  handling during remodeling, 94
  See also Tile, original floor

G

Gable end, 64, 65
Gables, adding headroom, *92*
Garages, detached, *112,* 117
Greene & Greene, 24, 135, 156

H

Hipped roof, 116
Historic review board, 182
Home library, *101*
Home office, 109, **109,** 110, *111*
Houses by Mail: A Guide to Houses from Sears, Roebuck and Company, 134

I

Inglenook, 14, *16*
Iowa Bungalow, *137, 166, 166, 167,* 168, *168, 169,* 170, **170,** *171,* 172, *172, 173*

J

Japanese style, 18, **21,** 140